ShopTalk

Ideas for Elementary School Librarians & Technology Specialists

Second Edition

Sharron L. McElmeel, Editor

D1558016

A Publication of THE BOOK REPORT & LIBRARY TALK
Professional Growth Series

Linworth Publishing, Inc.
Worthington, Ohio

Library of Congress Cataloging-in-Publication Data

Published by Linworth Publishing, Inc.
480 East Wilson Bridge Road, Suite L
Worthington, Ohio 43085

Copyright©2000 by Linworth Publishing, Inc.

Series Information:
    From The Professional Growth Series

ISBN 0-938865-94-3
5 4 3 2 1

Table of Contents

About the Editor

*S*harron L. McElmeel is a veteran educator who has learned much from her peers. She often teaches courses in literature and technology to her professional peers and to undergraduates who are entering the field of education. Much of her own writing is the result of requests made to her for information she has gathered about authors and illustrators. Among her many publications are ABCs of an Author/Illustrator Visit, Research Strategies for Moving Beyond Reporting, *and* Literature Frameworks: From Apples to Zoos—*all published by Linworth Publishing, Inc.*

Linworth Publishing, Inc. has also released the 3rd revision of Internet for Schools—*a book she co-authored with Carol Simpson; and* World Wide Web Almanac: Making Curriculum Connections to Special Days, Weeks, and Months *which she co-authored with Carol Smallwood.*

Sharron L. McElmeel was born in Cedar Rapids, Iowa, and obtained an undergraduate degree in education and later earned a Master's degree and pursued post-graduate work at the University of Iowa. For the past 25 years she has lived in a rural area of Linn County in Iowa where she shares her home with her husband and more than 10,000 books. When she is not writing she is enjoying her family— four sons, two daughters, and three grandchildren, reading, and her role of community activist. Visit her website at http://www.mcelmeel.com.

Introduction

The first edition of *ShopTalk* was published in 1994. At the time Linworth editors collected the contributions to the "ShopTalk" column published in each edition of *LIBRARY TALK: The Magazine for Elementary School Library Media & Technology Specialists*, since its first issue. The book proved to be as popular as the column. Now this new compilation is being gleaned from contributions that have appeared in the "ShopTalk" column since 1994. All of the contributions have been included from *LIBRARY TALK*. Some items have been selected from the "Tips & Pointers" column that appeared for several years in *TECHNOLOGY CONNECTION*, which is now a popular section included in *LIBRARY TALK* and its sister publication *THE BOOK REPORT: The Magazine for Secondary School Library Media & Technology Specialists*.

Sharing with colleagues seems to be a hallmark of the specialists who deal with library media centers and with technology. Testimony to this is the heavy traffic on LM_NET <http://ericir.syr.edu/lm_net/>, which is a virtual sharing forum for school library media specialists. That listserv and the many contributions to the "ShopTalk" column are ample evidence that we are a sharing group.

Not all of the ideas will be new to all readers, but each item will be new to someone. Some of the ideas are even similar-but with a little different twist or focus. We included those as well. It is difficult to guess which idea or what twist will spark an adaptation that you can use. Will the tip about taking pictures of student teachers to help them develop their professional portfolio inspire you to update your own resumé and perhaps begin to take some pictures in your classroom for a portfolio of your accomplishments? Or perhaps

the tip about creating a threefold brochure on the computer will get you thinking about creating one for your library media center. A tip in the column about using author pictures near their books in the library gave me the idea to establish an "Author's Gallery." Each year when our featured author or authors visit the school I take pictures of them. Later I select a close-up to enlarge to an eight- by 10-inch photo, and have it matted and framed. A $3 engraved plate with the author's name and the date is attached, and the picture is hung in a prominent area of the library.

Sometimes the hint will be one that you cannot use at all because the equipment required is not available to you, and a comparable hint is not included for the equipment you do have. However, even in those situations, the tip may lead you to ask others who are perhaps more experienced with your particular equipment if that function is available to you. For example, in one hint, the keystrokes are given to capture a screen shot using a Macintosh computer. Similar information is not included for the PC, but certainly there is a way that an image of the screen can be captured to print for handouts and manuals to use with your students. A little checking with others may help you find the answer. Without the tip, you might not have ever asked the question- and would never have known that it could be done.

Each idea may be new to you and a perfect fit, or it may be an idea that you have known about for a while. Of the more than 400 ideas in this compilation, many are bound to be ideas you can use or tips that spark great new adaptations appropriate to your situation.

There are eight sections in this book. Just as it is difficult to catalog a book when it is equally appropriate in two distinct areas, so, too, was it difficult to categorize many of the hints. We were able to identify eight basic strands: bulletin boards, curriculum connections, promoting reading, teaching library skills, managing the library, public relations, using technology in the classroom, and technology talk—a section focusing on the "management" of technology more than its use for instruction. Each of the contributions fit in one of the strands quite nicely, however some could easily have been placed in two, and sometimes three, sections. When an idea sparks an adaptation that fits your situation a little bit better, keep in mind that your variation on a good idea may spark yet another variation for someone else. It's worth sharing. Consider sending along your idea to be published in *LIBRARY TALK*. You may send ideas to <linworth@linworth.com>. Be sure to put "shop talk" in the subject line. If your hint is published a surprise thank you will be sent your way. We'll look to see your ideas in print.

Sharron L. McElmeel, Editor

Putting Your Best Image Forward – Bulletin Boards and Displays

> # When I walk into a school and see a good library,
> # it usually means that there's a good principal.
>
> *Jean Fritz, 1985*

The image the school and media center puts forth to those who visit gives an impression of the quality of the people and the quality of the program in that school. A friendly and productive learning environment should be their first impression. Eye-catching displays, green plants, fresh bulletin boards, and an uncluttered work area will all contribute to the "good library" image. A few years ago our library media center was scheduled to have new carpet installed. It was the impetus to give our media center a new look.

Our metal beige bookshelves were scratched and tired looking. We thought about new wood shelves but found the cost prohibitive. Instead, we declared a painting day and marbleized the end caps of the shelves with three colors that would bring out colors from the carpet. The can for shelf markers was decorated to match as were the ends of the book carts and wastebaskets. A few potted seasonal flowers sat on the study tables, green plants sat among the books in the display cabinets, and hanging baskets of English Ivy hung near the southern exposure windows. We purchased a couple of inexpensive solid-colored plush area carpets to put in front of the circulation desk and near a large oak cabinet in the reading area.

The result was smashing. The plants were donated, the carpets purchased at a school discount, and the paint costs were minimal. The total renovation cost less than $50, and was funded by the school's Parent Teachers Association (PTA). Seldom did anyone enter the media center without commenting on what a pleasant learning environment the center seemed to be. It is first impressions that invite young learners in, but it is your program that keeps them wanting to come back. Here are some tried-and-true hints for creating a space that puts your center's best image forward.

Bulletin Boards and Displays

15-Minute Bulletin Boards

Cover the background of a large bulletin board with maps, such as the kind that often come in *National Geographic*, or just state maps. In large letters spread the phrase "READING TAKES YOU PLACES" across the surface of these maps—as if "traveling" across them. Another idea, cover the bulletin board with newspapers and covers from magazines. On top of these, attach the phrase "READ PERIODICALLY."

— *Kay Whisler, Tinora Junior High, Defiance, Ohio*

A Castle on a Bookshelf

We made a structure that looks like a castle wall with towers, painted it bright yellow and red, and put it on the top of some library shelves. Book characters peek over the walls and out the windows. We change them every nine weeks. It has been a fun way to brighten an old library.

— *Trudy Doll, Clearwater (Kansas) Elementary School*

An Album of Bulletin Boards

The library aide gave me a small photo album and helps me take pictures of our bulletin boards throughout the year. It's fun to take this to meetings, and it helps us remember ideas and how we used them.

— *Trudy Doll, Clearwater (Kansas) Elementary School*

Author Focus

Provide an eye-catching focus on your author/illustrator bulletin boards by featuring a poster-sized reproduction of the author/illustrator. We obtain photographs from publishers' brochures about authors, reference books that feature reproducible photographs, or pictures we have taken. The photos are taken to a local photography shop and enlarged into a poster-size picture. We surround the giant photo with book jackets or posters featuring that author's books. This makes the author corner in the library something special.

— *Sharron L. McElmeel*

Banners

Put Print Shop or any other banner-making program to good use. Make banners promoting special or frequently used URLs. The banners can then be used to decorate your lab or media center.

— *Mary Alice Anderson, Winona (Minnesota) Middle School*

Board Contests

We have several bulletin boards in our library. I have placed posters on the boards and asked different grades to suggest a library-related slogan or caption for the posters. It has evolved into a contest for the third, fourth, and fifth grades. Winners are given an inexpensive book bag.

— Rita Schluter, Maercker Elementary School, Westmont, Illinois

Book Character Pumpkins

For Halloween, we put a different twist on decorating pumpkins by encouraging children to portray characters from children's books. We provided scraps of felt, construction paper, yarn, glitter, and other things that inspire crafts. We suggested that children bring in articles of clothing or parts of old Halloween costumes. As an example, I made a Velveteen Rabbit pumpkin with ears cut from textured wallpaper and whiskers from pipe cleaners. You can be sure that children will want to make pumpkins dressed as Little Red Riding Hood, the Cat in the Hat, and other popular characters.

— Andrea Troisi, LaSalle Middle School, Niagara Falls, New York

Bulletin Boards by Class

To help students feel some ownership in the media center, I ask each class to put up a bulletin board. The class members and I brainstorm ideas and choose one. The children put the items up themselves. I start the year with the oldest students first. Each board is up for two weeks.

— Paula S. Bradway, Prairie Heights Elementary School, Cedar Rapids, Iowa

Candid Camera

I keep an inexpensive instant camera in my desk for those special library moments that cannot be staged. When the photos are developed, I select the best ones for enlarging and make a special display. Kids love to see themselves in a positive situation.

— Evelyn Hammaren, Randolph (New Jersey) High School

Car Tags for the States

I made a sign from a car license plate to identify books about our state, Kansas. I enlarged the Dewey number with a software program and then cut the number to fit on a Kansas tag, leaving the state name visible. The plate can be hung or placed on the shelf with the books. I put a vase of sunflowers (our state flower) by the sign.

— Rebecca Mavity, Garfield Elementary School, Ottawa, Kansas

CD-ROM Border

Back "issues" of CD-ROMs make a nice border for a bulletin board or other display. Just string them together with yarn, and they become a 90s-style border. And they are attention getting.

— *Mary Alice Anderson, Winona (Minnesota) Middle School*

Holiday Decorations from Quilt Batting

We made fluffy snowflakes and snowmen for holiday decorations by cutting the shapes from quilt batting. To keep the batting from sliding while we cut it, we sandwiched it between sheets of thin paper.

— *Beverly Budzynski, Grand Blanc (Michigan) Middle School*

Homemade Magnetic Storyboard

I use a metal kitchen countertop protector as a magnetic storyboard. Any number of magnetic items can be used for the story characters, including commercial or "teacher made" items with magnetic tape attached, toy alphabet letters, or kitchen magnets. The kitchen magnets have been the most surprising success. Dinosaurs, animals, and cartoon figures are favorites. A spur-of-the-moment purchase—magnets in the shapes of grocery carts, mixers, egg cartons, hot dogs, and muffins—has been especially popular.

— *Iris T. Collins, Harrison Central Elementary School, Gulfport, Mississippi*

Inexpensive Bulletin Board Backgrounds

Do you have a large bulletin board to decorate? Mine is seven feet wide by four feet long. A disposable vinyl tablecloth makes an inexpensive, seamless background. The tablecloths are available in many colors and can easily be trimmed to the needed size.

— *Arlene Kachka, Holy Trinity High School, Chicago, Illinois*

National Library Week Quilt

For National Library Week, I cut eight-inch squares of cotton for each student in our school. Using magic markers or crayons, the students drew a picture about reading, the library, or a favorite book. A volunteer sewed the squares together, making two quilts. A group of quilters brought their frame to the library and helped the children tie their squares. The finished products now hang on a rod in the library.

— *Shirley Seizer, Sacred Heart Elementary School, Spencer, Iowa*

Old Photos and Favorite Books

A display of photos of teachers and other staff members when they were babies or young children fascinated our students. Each photo was captioned with the teachers' comments about a favorite childhood book. The students had a lot of fun trying to guess who was pictured. If you display the favorite books beside the photo display, you'll receive many requests for the books.

— *Diane Briggs, Maplewood School, Watervliet, New York*

Recycle the Card Catalog, Drawers and All

We recycled the old card catalog by converting the drawers to planters. You can buy plastic liners to fit the drawers so that you can fill them with plants, real or artificial. The cabinet itself can be recycled for a display area by removing the drawer dividers, painting the interior, and adding a light fixture. We also added a hinged door with a glass pane. Finally, for the cards themselves, we sent selected cards to the appropriate authors requesting an autograph.

— *Barbara Bluestein, Princeton High School, Cincinnati, Ohio*

[Editor's Note: Consider sending two cards to each author and donating the second autographed catalog card to your local reading or librarian's professional organizations to be auctioned or raffled at their next convention.]

Transparent Snowflakes & Other Things

If you have a roll laminator, you know that there is always "wasted" film at the beginning of each use. We use the Ellison Lettering Machine to cut snowflake shapes from the transparent film. Then, with a glue stick, children add glitter to the flakes for a wintertime decoration.

— *Beverly Budzynski, Grand Blanc (Michigan) Middle School*

SECTION 2

Connecting
with the Curriculum

> **Education is a social process... Education is growth...
> Education is not a preparation for life; education is life itself.**
>
> *John Dewey (1859-1952)*

The library media center has the resources to help teachers and children make connections to the curriculum-resources that will enhance learning in all subjects of the curriculum. This is accomplished by creating links—connections—between these resources and all subject areas from one to another. The primary goal of any effective curriculum is to help students develop the skills and strategies they need to become independent learners. These connection ideas will help introduce curriculum units, clarify concepts, and motivate interests in areas students might not have otherwise explored. Think of these ideas as prototypes for developing additional connections that you can make.

Art: Contests for the Very Young

We held six art contests last year, three for upper elementary grades (3-5) and three for the lower grades. To enter, students read a book or story in a genre or by a certain author and made an illustration using the three primary colors. For the lower elementary grades, the categories were fairy tales, nursery rhymes, and Dr. Seuss. For the upper grades, they were Laura Ingalls Wilder, Roald Dahl, and Shel Silverstein. In coming years we will do just two contests so students won't get bored or burned out with the idea. Our library and school hallways look especially pretty with the framed drawings.

— *Gail Shulman & Kay Gibson, Grand Blanc Community Schools, Flint, Michigan*

Collaboration: Create an Internet Projects Notebook

I created an Internet Projects notebook for keeping track of the ideas that come over the listservs. I arrange projects alphabetically by title, with the subject line highlighted for easy identification, and notify teachers of new project ideas through the media center newsletter. As projects expire, or I see no interest, I remove them from the notebook.

— *Shelley Glantz, Arlington (Massachusetts) High School*

Collaboration: Facts on Sticky Notes

When students hunt for facts, they write the facts on sticky notes and attach these notes to their worksheets. The colorful sticky notes seem to make the assignment fun.

— *Gayle Schmuhl, Ford Middle School, Brook Park, Ohio*

Collaboration: For Best Results

Before introducing a new idea or reference skill to students, go over the lesson in advance with the classroom teacher. The teacher will understand what is going on and will be able to help answer students' questions when the lesson is presented.

— *Steve Baule, Glenbrook South High School, Glenview, Illinois*

Collaboration: Library Skills Lessons to Link Classroom Needs

To meet the needs of my teaching staff, I pulled together all the handouts I created for skills lessons throughout the year. From this great pile of stuff, I put together skills booklets for fourth, fifth, and sixth grades on topics such as orientation, locating information, reference skills, and booktalks. My district paid to have one booklet printed for each student. Each fall, I give a copy of the appropriate booklet to each teacher and ask him or her to tell me when specific skills need to be taught to support their class work. Because I've organized my materials, I'm prepared to teach the skills on short notice and to always link my lessons to classroom needs. I don't have to keep track of who's done what—I just check their booklets to see if a certain class needs me to teach a particular topic.

— *Jacque Burkhalter, Fidalgo Elementary School, Anacortes, Washington*

Collaboration: Picture Books for Teachers

It seemed that every time a teacher searched the shelves for a specific picture book, it was either checked out or nearly worn out. To help solve the problem, I set up a reserve area for teachers. I use a small percentage of my budget to order a second copy of frequently requested books that support the language arts and math curriculums. A "teacher copy" label is placed on the covers of the books, and they are shelved in the professional books section. The teachers like this idea.

— *Valerie Wolny, Knollwood School, Decatur, Georgia*

Collaboration: Project Reminders

In one elementary school media center, the librarian uses a loose-leaf binder to keep a record of what each teacher's class is working on. The materials are indexed by the teachers' names. Handouts of guidelines along with the librarian's notes are kept in the binders. In this way, a quick glance tells the librarian what has already been done and what she needs to prepare for.

— *Sandra Jull, Spalding University, Louisville, Kentucky*

Collaboration: Research Projects Linked to The Big Six

All research projects are linked to The Big Six, a research process developed by Michael Eisenberg and Robert Berkowitz of Syracuse University. Media center use has increased; kids know their way around the media center; the demand for books is up; and all research projects are sensational!

— *Janis V. Isenberg, Middlebrook Elementary School, Trumbull, Connecticut*

[Editor's Note: Learn more about Eisenberg and Berkowitz's strategies by visiting <http://www.Big6.com/>.]

Collaboration: Working Cooperatively

Librarians and teachers are natural partners when it comes to teaching research. I split the class with the classroom teacher, who works with students to explain the assignment procedures: narrow topic, outline ideas, show examples. In the meantime, I teach search skills, including Boolean, truncation, and keyword search difficulties (e.g., variant spellings, synonyms, plurals), and show how the appropriate programs operate. Then we switch groups. After the initial two or three class periods, intermediate or middle school students will be ready to do their research.

— *Lois McNicol, Garney Valley High School, Glen Mills, Pennsylvania*

Mathematics: How Much Is a Yak Worth?

For a contest during National Book Week, students were challenged to find the names of animals and practice their math. On a worksheet we assigned point values for letters of the alphabet. Each letter from A-H was worth one point; from I-Q, 10 points; and from R-Z, 100 points. As an example, we showed that with a y worth 100 points, an *a* one point, and a *k* 10 points, the word *yak* was worth 111 points. Then, we asked students to find an animal that was worth more than a yak in points. The student who found an animal's name worth the most points won the prize. Students had to show their addition. They could enter as many times as they wanted. Authors' names or book titles could be used instead of animal names.

— *Cindy Cox, Oakwood Elementary School, Hickory, North Carolina*

Mathematics: Meet a Mathematician

"Conversations with Famous International Mathematicians" is a multicultural and research project that the math teachers and I have used with elementary and middle school students. Each child selects one mathematician and researches his or her life and contributions to the science. The children then present their findings by acting out a scene from the mathematician's life. Parent volunteers have helped with costumes and videotaping. I presented this project at a meeting of the International Association of School Librarianship in Belfast, Ireland.

— Madeleine M. Hoss, Metcalf Laboratory School, Normal, Illinois

Mathematics: Serious Kindergarten (and Early Primary) Polling

I quickly learned that voting for a favorite book could be hilarious fun for kindergarten children. They raised their hands for every book I showed them. My solution was to set each book on a chair or bookshelf top and have children stand in front of the book they wanted to vote for.

— Cindy Cox, Oakwood Elementary School Hickory, North Carolina

[Editor's note: This is a great preliminary activity for creating a bar graph. Recreate the "human" bar graph on a large sheet of butcher paper. Use a photocopy of the book jacket and a copy of the child's school picture to replicate the voting.]

Reading—Safety: Officer Buckle's Star

After hearing the 1996 Caldecott Winner, Officer Buckle and Gloria (Putnam), second graders decorated a star with a safety tip and a drawing. We posted the "stars" on our bulletin board, which was captioned "Officer Buckle's Safety Tips." If this activity is used in October, Halloween safety rules could be included or the activity could be incorporated into a unit on fire safety, bus safety, or personal safety.

— Audrey Nolte, Richland Elementary School, Quakertown, Pennsylvania

Reading—Vocabulary: What Does It Mean?

Try increasing vocabulary awareness by posting a new word and its definition each week. Make a poster reading, "And You Said [insert vocabulary word] Means What? [insert definition]." The poster is laminated. Rubber cement is used to post the vocabulary word and its definition, which are written in contrasting colors. Vocabulary words can be taken from textbooks and vocabulary games.

— Dorothy Turner, Pepperell Middle School, Lindale, Georgia

Reading/Writing: Thumbs-Up Reviews for Beginning Readers

As new books are unpacked, I set aside picture books and their jackets for fifth graders to review. The project is divided into two sessions. In the first session, I explain to the fifth graders the purpose of a book review and share examples of printed reviews. We then discuss how our younger students who aren't able to read these reviews would still like to know which books others think are good. Working in pairs, the fifth graders then select a new picture book to read and review.

In the second session, the students rate the illustrations, story setting, and characters on a scale from one to three. Books with a total score of eight or above receive a thumbs-up; those with a total score below eight receive a thumbs-down. I use Print Shop software to create the thumb symbol. The ratings sheet and thumb are taped to the book jackets. Completed reviews are hung in the hallway outside the library where younger students, parents, and teachers can see them. The reviewed books are displayed on top of the shelves where they can be easily located by the cover. The weeks following this project are some of the media center's busiest!

— *Mary Jane Michels, James H. Hendrix Elementary School, Inman, South Carolina*

[Editor's Note: Consider having the older readers take their reviews "on the road" to visit primary classes and present their review orally. Using the popular movie review television segments as a prototype, videotape book review segments to be aired in primary classrooms or checked out for parent and child use at home.]

Reading: The "Art" of Reading

To spark children's interest in illustrators, I introduce the children to artistic styles that they can try in the library or classroom. Eric Carle, who works in collage, is a favorite subject. One week I read a few of his books to the children, pointing out the style of his illustrations. The next week the students and I read *Draw Me a Star*, and then we do just that. The students each have paper, scissors, and paste to create their own collage stars. Their work is displayed in the library.

— *Allison Bernstein, Wayland (Massachusetts) High School*

[Editor's Note: Consider collaborating with your school's art teacher on this project. You introduce and discuss the examples. The art teacher revisits the examples and teaches the art technique. Use Brian Pinkney's art for scratchboard, Craig Brown's for stippling, Patricia Polacco's for watercolor, and so forth.]

Reading: Transparent Puppets

Puppet plays can be produced using the overhead projector to cast characters onto the screen. Make a black-and-white drawing of story characters and use the drawing to create an overhead transparency. Then color the figures, using transparency markers, and cut them out to produce the actors for the play.

— *Sharron L. McElmeel*

Science: How's the Weather?

Written and illustrated by Claire Henley, *Stormy Day* (Hyperion, 1992) and *Sunny Day* (Hyperion, 1992) are excellent books to use in a discussion of weather. Each book features vivid illustrations, a simple text, and a sense of the familiar. *Stormy Day* captures the sounds of a summer thunderstorm, the frolicking of children in puddles, and the glistening of a rainbow—all the things that make a stormy day fun and exciting. *Sunny Day* provides a look at warm weather pleasures, such as relaxing in a hammock, splashing in the waves at the shore, or enjoying ice cream cones at the beach. Divide the class into two groups, and assign one group to write and illustrate an account of how to spend a stormy day. Have the other group concentrate on what to do on a sunny day. After each group has written and illustrated its book, display the finished products in the school's library media center next to a display of books on weather. As a culminating experience in the classroom, read *The Snowy Day* by Ezra Jack Keats to give students a preview of what delights to expect when winter comes.

— *Andrea Troisi, LaSalle Middle School, Niagara Falls, New York*

Science: Shoe Box Kits

The Science Corner in our media center features books from our 500s collection and more than 50 experiments packaged for circulation in plastic shoe boxes. The "shoe box science kits" may be checked out for two days. Volunteer mothers check in the kits and restock them. This fall we added rotating "live" science exhibits. Exhibits have included cocoons that opened to butterflies, a lizard, and a miniature human skeleton. After the exhibits were added, students quickly checked out books relating to butterflies, lizards, and the human body. A few of the volunteers plan to loan their children's unusual pets for future exhibits.

— *Sally Ray, Wells Elementary School, Plano, Texas*

Social Studies—Geography: Cookie Cutter Center

I have several activity centers in our K-grade 3 library. One is the "Create-a-Bookmark" center where cookie cutters of all shapes are available. Children like to trace realistic-looking forms and shapes for their bookmarks, and cookie cutters are the answer. Another center is called "Explore the World." A world map is on display. Beside the map I post a section of the daily newspaper called "World Today." I circle the country names in blue and the cities in red. If students can find these places on the map, I give them a sticker.

— *Iris T. Collins, Harrison Central Elementary School, Gulfport, Mississippi*

Social Studies: 50 States Data—On the Road with Databases

Using the three databases available on our network, I created a set of questions on each of the 50 states and then presented students with a "question of the week." The students put cards containing their name, their answer, and the source they used into a box, and I held a weekly drawing. The first entry drawn with the correct answer received a small prize. In the media center, I displayed a large U.S. map with a small car that traveled from state to state as the questions were answered. Students used an atlas program to determine how many miles our little car had traveled each week.

— *Kristy Patterson, Callaway Middle School, Hogansville, Georgia*

Social Studies: Cultural Diversity

Our sixth grade students researched countries as part of our year-long theme "Celebrating Our Cultural Diversity." As an added touch, the students learned to enter the final reports on the computer and to use computer graphics to design a cover. The results were so impressive that the finished products were displayed at the public library.

— *Elizabeth Garbarino, Riverhead (New York) Middle School*

Social Studies: Family Studies-Multicultural Me

"Multicultural Me" is a project that the library initiated, and the entire school participated in. I posted a large map of the world in the central hallway, gave each student a "family tree" form, and asked him or her to discuss with parents and grandparents their family's cultural/ethnic heritage. Each student chose one country of ancestry and wrote the name of the country on a miniature American flag. The flags were placed around the map. Later, we stapled red yarn from each country of ancestry to the collection of flags from students' background. A food fair, displays of family memorabilia, and grandparents' visits to the school throughout the year, are continuations of the Multicultural Me program.

— *Sheila Miller, East Pike Elementary School, Indiana, Pennsylvania*

Social Studies: Geography and Storytime

I use library storytime (at all grade levels) as an opportunity to promote geography with my students. A world map and an U.S. map are on display at all times. Whenever possible, I point out and talk about where a story takes place or where an author or illustrator lives.

— *Juneal Reitan, McAuliffe Elementary School, McAllen, Texas.*

Social Studies: News in Education

During American Education week, our guest was the News in Education (NIE) coordinator from our local newspaper. The children participated in "Treasure Hunt," an educational game. They were divided into groups of five, and each group selected a leader and a recorder. The object of the game was to cross five "information barriers" to reach a treasure. Each barrier could be surmounted with information from the newspaper. They had to use items or services found in the retail or classified ads in the newspaper. The game used computation, creativity, research, group dynamics, verbal presentation, and problem solving skills. For more information, contact the NIE coordinator at your local newspaper.

— *Madeleine M. Hoss, Metcalf Laboratory School, Normal, Illinois*

Social Studies: Passports to See the World

In collaboration with the fifth grade social studies teacher, we involved students in research and multicultural studies. After researching a country, students made a collage poster and filled their "passports" with highlights of their research. As a culminating activity, a parent cooked a dish from one of the countries, and students and parents sampled different kinds of breads. Other parents were invited to attend the activity and ask students about their research.

— *Madeleine M. Hoss, Metcalf Laboratory School, Normal, Illinois*

Social Studies: Promoting Philately-The Collection and Study of Postage Stamps and Postal Stationery

You can easily introduce students to stamp collecting by asking the school secretaries, and those in the central administrative offices, to save stamps or the entire envelopes from incoming mail. Give the stamps to students who have a collection or to those who are interested in starting one. Use some of the stamps in displays to encourage students to find out more about the person or situation depicted on the stamps.

— *Anitra Gordon, Lincoln High School, Ypsilanti, Michigan*

[Editor's Note: For all types of information about stamps and stamp collecting make a World Wide Web visit to <http://www.linns.com>—Linn's Stamp News Online: The Internet Source for Stamp Collecting Online]

Social Studies: White House E-Mail Addresses

Students and teachers may write to Bill Clinton and Al Gore at these e-mail addresses: <president@whitehouse.gov> or <vice-president@whitehouse.gov>.

— *Beth Farris, Cummings Elementary School, Memphis, Tennessee*

Spelling: Tapes for Practice

Help children practice their weekly spelling words by recording them on an audiocassette tape. Say the word number, pronounce the word, use the word in a sentence, and pronounce the word again. Wait 10 seconds, then pronounce the word, spell the word slowly, and pronounce the word again. Use a timer to allow enough time between words. Place the tape in a listening center for children to use throughout the week to prepare for the final test.

— *Sharron L. McElmeel*

SECTION 3

Focus on Reading

> ## The man who does not read good books has not advantage over the man who can't read them.
>
> *Mark Twain (1835-1910)*

More than a decade ago the National Academy of Education's Commission on Reading issued a highly publicized report, *Becoming a Nation of Readers*. Citing the importance of access to interesting and informative books, the report suggested that young learners need to have an adequate selection of books from which to choose, and the most important role of an educator is to encourage wide reading and to help match books to children. In your role of encouraging reading, here are some tips that just may work for you.

"Neat Kid" Award

In addition to the books checked out by children in a class, I check out an extra book to the student named a "neat kid" by his teacher. The student is chosen for his classroom behavior, such as returning homework on time or remembering to raise his hand before speaking. The extra book is often a new one, and I booktalk it for the whole class before giving it to the student.

— *Nancy Turner, Westcreek Elementary School, Fort Worth, Texas*

A Hard-to-Win Contest

Here's a contest for teachers that's made possible by automated circulation systems. With many automation systems, for example, Circulation Plus or Winnebago to name just two, class lists can be printed showing the number of books checked out by individual students from the beginning of the school year. I ask teachers to guess which student in their class checked out the most books. Notice that I did not say who read the most books. It is seldom that a teacher guesses the correct student. When I do need to give a prize, I use free paperbacks from book fair profits.

— *Cindy Cox, Oakwood Elementary School, Hickory, North Carolina*

[Editor's Note: This is a great way to encourage teachers to actually look at the statistics about students and their reading habits. In addition to alerting teachers to those students who may need to be encouraged to visit the library media center more regularly, the information can be used with parents during parent-teacher conferences to assist in the evaluation of the child's reading habits.]

A Jumanji Board

While working with second graders, I did an author study of Chris Van Allsburg. We read his books and discussed his artwork. Working in pairs, the students designed the spaces for a large *Jumanji* board. An example: "This tiger is definitely not stuffed—move back three spaces." After assembling the three- by seven-foot game board, we began work on our own story, using the spaces the students designed.

— Allison Trent Bernstein, Blake Middle School, Medfield, Massachusetts

BEAR Pairs

Our library theme revolves around BEARS (Be Enthusiastic About Reading). As part of the theme, we pair an upper-grade class with a lower grade and call them BEAR Buddy Classes. The children work together on various projects. For example, the two classes come to the media center at the same time so that the older students can help the younger ones select books. Afterward, the pairs sit down to read together.

— Leslie Pratschler, B.C. Haynie Elementary School, Jonesboro, Georgia

Birthday Bear Books

Not only does our library add more than 200 new books annually, but thanks to a donation program known as Birthday Bear, we also have a built-in opportunity to promote books and reading. Parents and grandparents donate the price of a book in recognition of a child's birthday. The child is recognized on the book's donor plate, on the morning announcements, and in our library newsletter. But, the best promotion is reading the book to the child's class. I take the book and a stuffed bear to the honoree's class. The teachers have agreed to drop everything when I show up. If the book is longer than a picture book, I read the jacket blurb and the first chapter. The birthday child can be the first to check out the book.

— Pat Miller, Walker Station Elementary School, Sugar Land, Texas

Book Coupons for Teachers-Promoting the Professional Collection

To encourage our teachers to make more use of our professional collection, I inserted several coupons deep within the pages of some of the books. Each coupon entitled the finder to a book of her choice from any book fair at the school. Since the book fair companies give a percentage of gross sales in free books, there was no cost to the library. I put the coupons on Post-It notes so they would not fall out of the books.

— Owen Ditchfield, Edward A. White Elementary School, Fort Benning, Georgia

Breakfast Book Club

Our Breakfast Book Club meets in the library on the first Thursday morning of each month. We discuss a paperback from the library's collection that we have all read or books by the same author. Last year about 12 fifth and sixth graders joined. This year, the 31 students joined. The principal supports us by providing funds for the breakfast of muffins and juice.

— *Sheila Miller, East Pike School, Indiana, Pennsylvania*

Capture Readers

Keep an inexpensive disposable camera close at hand and take photographs of readers in the library media center and in reading class. Feature the photographs on a "Readers Are Leaders" bulletin board.

— *Sharron L. McElmeel*

Coupons for Book Characters

On Halloween, students are asked to dress up as book characters instead of donning the traditional scary costumes. To encourage staff members to participate, we give each teacher who comes as a book character a coupon for a free book at the book fair.

— *Margie Hall, Chapel Hill Elementary, Douglasville, Georgia*

Dewey Decimal Dash

Every year I challenge third and fourth grade students to read one book from each Dewey section of the nonfiction books plus a biography. I have laminated a generic chart to use in keeping records of their reading. After a class checks in books, those children who want to participate in the "dash" stand by the chart. I ask them simple questions such as "What did you learn that you didn't know?" Then I put a check in the appropriate column. Besides diversifying their reading choices, the "dash" acquaints them with the Dewey decimal system.

— *Ronda Nissen, Spring Bluff School, Winthrop Harbor, Illinois*

Reading Calendars

To promote reading outside the school, I distribute F.R.E.D. Calendars. The acronym F.R.E.D. stands for Families Reading Every Day. Each student is given a calendar to take home. Students are asked to read for 15 minutes each day and to record it on the calendar. Parents, siblings, and grandparents can also participate in the project. The reading must be done at home. Each child keeps the calendar for one month. Teachers support the project by including F.R.E.D. reading as a homework assignment and keeping calendars themselves. The first year I tried this project, 90 calendars were returned; the next year, 125 calendars were returned.

— Cindy Cox, Oakwood Elementary School, Hickory, North Carolina

Finding Booktalk Gems on First Reading

I like to read excerpts from books when I do booktalks, but I don't like to thumb through each book looking for exciting paragraphs. I've started a new filing system just for booktalks. When I read a book for the first time, I write the call number, author, and title on flue top of a three- by five-inch card. I use the card as a bookmark. When I come across an attention-grabbing passage or picture, I write the page number on the card. When I've finished the book, I file the cards according to genre or call number.

— Nancy Phillips, Farwell Elementary School, Spokane, Washington

First-Come, First-Served Booktalks

I was frustrated by the number of students who failed to come to the library to check out books they had reserved after hearing booktalks. Now, after booktalks, I display the covers on a bulletin board. The books can be checked out on Fridays, first-come, first-served. Even students who missed the booktalks will ask for the "Friday" books.

— Mimi Malis, Covington Middle School, Austin, Texas

Good Book Endorsements

Before the circulation system was automated, students often read a book's check-out card to see if their friends had read it and might recommend it. We've found a way to continue these "informal endorsements" even though the system is now automated. We put cards and pockets in the books and invite students to sign the cards of books they would recommend to others.

— Sue Dalelio, Downtown Elementary School, Columbus, Georgia

Great Display

A disposable camera is a useful item to have at school. When you spot a student or staff member reading in the cafeteria, on the playground, in the library, or any other interesting location pull out your camera to take a picture. Develop the photographs at a photo service that offers a two for the price of one print option. Give a copy to each subject and use your copies to create an ever changing "Interesting Places to Read" display. This not only promotes reading but also encourages those who read.

— *Sharron L. McElmeel*

Halloween & Reading

A good way to celebrate at Halloween and be sensitive to parents who are concerned about the holiday's connotations is to designate the last week of October as Reading Week. Have students predict how many total pages they think their class can read in one week. Keep a record of pages read, and give small prizes to those whose prediction was the closest. On the last day of the month, ask children to come to school dressed as a favorite book character.

— *Terra Murphy, Spalding University, Louisville, Kentucky*

Jokes & Riddles Jar

A large jar, once used for pickles, sits at the entrance to the library. It now holds jokes and riddles written on slips of paper by students and teachers. Frequently I pull out a joke or riddle and read it to a class visiting the library. If the student who submitted the riddle stumps the class, he gets to choose a prize from our treasure chest. However, if another student guesses the answer, that student gets the prize. Joke and riddle books are always in demand.

— *Phyllis L. Mays, Code Elementary School, Seneca, South Carolina*

Local Celebrity Readers

To promote reading among our students, we asked the adults in our community, including local merchants, clergymen, chamber of commerce members, and members of the school staff to write a 150-word statement about what reading meant to them. We took color photographs of each participant and made posters for National Library Week. Our students showed a great interest in the posters because most of the faces were familiar.

— *Donna Brennan, Clarke Middle School, Westbury, New York*

Nonfiction for the Emerging Reader

Because the easy fiction section doesn't meet all first graders' needs for information, I put blue tape on books in the nonfiction section that are on the children's reading level. This helps them find books they can read in the "big kids' section."

— *Joan Crawford, UMS-Wright Preparatory School, Mobile, Alabama*

Pick and Stick

An activity we call "pick and stick" involves children picking a book to read for a 10-minute period and using a shelf marker (the "stick") to keep the book's place on the shelf. The children also pick where they sit to read—on the floor, under a table, in a corner, and so on. After 10 minutes, we have a two-minute period for standing up, stretching, and picking out another book for another reading session.

— *Sheila Miller, East Pike Elementary School, Indiana, Pennsylvania*

[Editor's Note: This 10-minute reading blitz will serve well to introduce young readers to a variety of books that they may wish to check out to finish reading.]

Post-Halloween Read-In

The day after Halloween trick-or-treat night, when children are tired from scouring their neighborhoods for candies, our school stages "Drop Everything and Read" day. Children may bring sleeping bags or blankets and a pillow to school, and desks are pushed aside. The focus is on reading, but we offer other activities related to reading. Primary teachers, especially, wanted to provide a variety of activities to keep their students interested. The activities we've used include guest readers from the community, buddy reading, decorating grocery bags or tray covers with pictures of book characters, and games and contests that feature books. A game that our students like is a takeoff on the early TV show *To Tell the Truth*. Teams of three students choose a book that only one of the three has read. The reader tells the story to the other two students, but all claim they have read the book when they appear before a class. After asking questions of all three, the audience guesses who read the book. We also make buttons from small pictures of book jackets, cut from publishers' catalogs and advertisements. The child who can give the title and a summary of the book gets to keep the button.

— *Shauna Leigh Udell, Virginia Peterson Elementary School, Paso Robles, California*

Prize Winner Books

A fun way to get students to go to books other than those associated with reading testing programs, such as the Accelerated Reader (AR) program, is to create a patron named "Prize Winner" in your computer. Then check out several books to Prize Winner. When a student tries to check out that book, the computer says it is checked out to Prize Winner, and the student gets a prize. I let the student select a book from those I got free from the book fair. I started this activity during National Children's Book Week, but it lasted until Christmas last year when the last book was found. The students really enjoy the activity, and I like it because it gets students to some of the other good books that are not on the AR list.

— *Wanda Nail, Northwest Primary School, Hereford, Texas*

Putting Teachers on Posters

To promote reading, I take pictures of teachers reading books and have them reproduced as posters. I make sure the book is a well-known one and the title is clearly visible in the photograph. I tape the posters on the library windows with the caption "Read and Succeed!" Students enjoy seeing pictures of their teachers reading.

— *Nancy Turner, Westcreek Elementary School, Fort Worth, Texas*

Reading Incentive Program

Our library features California Young Reader Medal books for our yearlong reading incentive program. All books are on display and have been marked with various colored seals and the date the book won or was nominated. We have primary, intermediate, and some middle school books. Each month a different activity is posted in the library and classrooms. Children read one of the books they have never read before, do the activity, and bring it to the library by the deadline. Activities are displayed and prizes are awarded each month. We will have a party at the end of the year for everyone who has participated at least once during the school year.

— *Nancy Heil, Prestwood Elementary School, Sonoma, California*

Reading Links Us to the World

A school-wide reading incentive program was titled "Reading Links Us to the World." Students who read a book about another country, set in another country, or about an ethnic group (other than their own) in this country received a paper link. The student's name and the book title were written on the link and added to a paper chain in the classroom. At the end of the program, the class in each grade with the most links won a special treat. Fifth graders read the most books with two classes finishing more than 700 titles. The local miniature golf course donated free passes, which we gave to the classes along with a novelty bookmark.

— *Sally Ray, Wells Elementary School, Plano, Texas*

Reading Motivator

A great reading motivator is using upper grades to read and interact with lower grades. Twice a year, I pair sixth graders with second graders, fifth graders with first graders, and third and fourth graders with kindergartners. They may go anywhere in the media center to read to each other. The younger children love to listen, and the older ones feel important and needed.

— *Cindy Black, East Side Elementary School, Harrisburg, Illinois*

Redwall Rewards

The favorite fantasy book in our library is *Redwall* by Brian Jacques (Putnam, 1987), but its length is intimidating to some middle school students. To motivate more students to try this book, I have printed buttons that read "I Made It Through the Wall—*Redwall*—351 Pages." As students read the book, they are awarded a button, and on the daily announcements, we proclaim: "Ten more students have made it through The Wall. Look for students wearing the buttons and ask them about it." We have seven copies, and there is a waiting list.

— *Louise Kehoe, Hemlock (Michigan) Middle School*

Sarah, Plain and Short

Because fourth graders read *Sarah, Plain and Tall* by Patricia MacLachlan (HarperCollins, 1985) in their language arts unit, they were treated to a visit from "Sarah, Plain and Short" (alias me, the librarian, dressed in a pioneer costume). As the children entered the "pioneer" library, they received a booklet titled *A Life on the Frontier* and looked at models of a covered wagon and a stagecoach. The children and I sat on quilts as I gave booktalks of fiction and nonfiction books about pioneer life. Library volunteers served donuts and juice. Later the children made reading quilts, which were displayed for American Education Week.

— *Elaine Orlick, Woodbridge (New Jersey) Township School District*

Student Jacket Artists

Students in grades 4-6 were asked to help "spruce up" the books in our collection that had little circulation appeal due to their relatively dull covers. After selecting and reading a book of their choice, students illustrated a new cover, complete with their names and classrooms as well as the author's name. Exceptional covers were placed in plastic protectors and affixed to the books, which were then returned to circulation. We have found that circulation of these books has increased since they were "re-covered."

— *Maryann E. Snail, St. Bernadette School, Monroeville, Pennsylvania*

Summer Library Hours

The parent-teacher group supported a summer school library program by paying staff for one hour a week. Neighborhood children were able to come to the school for book selection, storytelling, and a treat. Often preschool children attend as well as newly relocated families.

— *Liz Hunter, Hoover (Ohio) and Elizabethtown School*

The Old Book Game

Taking a cue from the child's game Old Maid, we have developed a game called Old Book. The rules are similar. Fifteen laminated cards show a picture and a word describing parts of a book, such as spine, cover, author, illustrator, and copyright date. Another 15 cards have only the pictures, no words. The 31st card of the deck is a ghastly looking creature named Old Book. To successfully complete a match, the student must define the term on his cards when he plays them. The student holding the Old Book... Well, you know the game.

— *Sherry A. Kalbach, Cornwall (Pennsylvania) Elementary School*

[Editor's Note: If you don't know how to play the Old Maid game you might visit <http://www.pagat.com>, which offers hot links to rules for several card games commonly played by children, including Old Maid.]

Wallpaper Quilts

Introduce students to a little-known aspect of the Civil War with Barbara Smucker's *Selina and the Bear Paw Quilt* (Crown, 1996). In the story, Mennonite farmers in Pennsylvania were persecuted because of their pacifist beliefs and refusal to fight. When Selina's family flees to Canada, her grandmother gives her a patchwork quilt that unites the generations. Give students wallpaper samples to replicate the bear paw patchwork and frame their illustrations for this story.

— *Andrea Troisi, LaSalle Middle School, Niagara Falls, New York*

SECTION 4

Library Skills
and the Curriculum

> ## School libraries should contain an abundance of what may be called collateral reading, relating to every part of the curriculum.
> *G.T. Little, 1896*

Developing an integrated curriculum is like weaving. The curriculum strands are of many colors, textures, and strengths and can be used as the warp threads. Library skills—the tools of learning—are the weft threads. The weft threads are woven in and out, over and under, and around the warp to create the tapestry of learning. Some of the suggestions provided below will provide just a hint of the tapestry—and suggest the curriculum colors and textures that should be woven with the library skills inherent in the suggestion. Each tapestry we suggest is sure to bring images of other tapestries you could create from curriculum and library skills threads popular in your school. Enjoy the weaving.

"Find Your Other Half"

As an aid to building a supportive library atmosphere for the learning of library skills, here is a fun activity for that first day in the library each school year. Using colorful illustrations from discarded books (or any other source), laminate the pictures if possible, mount them on heavier paper, and then cut them in half. Explain to your class that they are going to receive half an illustration, and they will have a few minutes to "find their other half." When they have a match, they are to talk with their partner and be prepared to introduce him or her to the group including information about what their partner likes to read, what their partner's favorite subjects are, if their partner has any pets, and so forth.

— *Betty Picone, Fredon Township School, Newton, New Jersey*

Alphabetical Order Aid

After watching young children stumble over alphabetical order as they searched for books in the card catalog. I ran a long piece of masking tape along the wooden strip at the top of the cabinet and printed the letters of the alphabet on the tape. Now children can clear up their confusion about alphabetical order quickly and independently by looking at the tape.

— *Sherry A. Kalback, Cornwall (Pennsylvania) Elementary School*

Alphabetizing Last Names

I found a way to use well-known authors' names in teaching alphabetical order to third graders. In an open space in the library, I placed five posters labeled A-E, F-J, K-O, P-T, and U-Z. After discussing alphabetizing by last name, I have the students alphabetize themselves by standing next to the poster where their last names would fit. Then I write three authors' full names on a small chalkboard and ask the children to alphabetize the authors' last names orally. We also talk about books the authors wrote.

— *Connie O. Scharre, Peachtree City (Georgia) Elementary School*

Atlas Lessons

After children have received one lesson on using an atlas, we have a reinforcement exercise the following week. Each group is given one atlas, a sheet of construction paper, and a marker. The students select a country and write four facts about it. Each group then presents its country to the class. Then I give some country facts at random to the class and all try to identify the country. Candies and pencils are given as awards.

— *Lois Weems, Rio Hondo (Texas) Elementary School*

"Catalog Cards" for Primary Students

I made "catalog cards," as a book location aid, by gluing book jacket fronts to construction paper, adding the appropriate call numbers, and laminating. With the card in hand, students more easily locate the book on the shelf. The cards can also be used to provide classes with some guided practice for locating books on the shelf.

— *Karen Whetzel, Ashby-Lee Elementary School, Mt. Jackson, Virginia*

Easter Egg Hunt for Books

Before the Easter holidays, third and fourth graders enjoy "hunting" for books to match call numbers concealed in plastic eggs. I place a basket of the eggs on the library counter. Inside each egg is a slip of paper with the call numbers of a book from the picture book, fiction, reference, biography, or nonfiction sections. Children who can locate the books receive jellybeans.

— *Martha Aucoin, Duson (Louisiana) Elementary School*

Find-the-Book Game

To aid in teaching location skills in the library media center, I have laminated cards on which call numbers for both fiction and nonfiction are written. When I have an extra five to 10 minutes at the end of a period, I pass out the cards. Students must bring me the books that match their cards. This activity also works as a team game, especially for grades 3-5.

— *Joan Crawford, UMS-Wright Preparatory School, Mobile, Alabama*

Function Key Identification

Our young (K-grade 5) students were familiar with Macintosh computers but not at all familiar with the IBM compatibles (or the function keys) that are used in our automated circulation system. The Winnebago circulation/catalog program uses the "F7" key to toggle the title, author, and subject screens. When children were reminded to use the F7 key, many pressed the "F" and the "7" keys. To solve the problem, we placed a blue dot (an adhesive sticker) above the F7 key on the keyboard. Now we remind those needing help to look for the "blue dot," and then press the F7 key below the dot. The blue dot works.

— Sharron L. McElmeel

Getting Acquainted in the Library

One of the first activities in the library involves a safari exploration. We send all 130 kindergarten and first grade students on an exploration of the library. Using bathroom tissue rolls (which I ask parents to save for us), we construct a pair of binoculars for each student. Two rolls are glued together side by side, and holes are punched for a cord. "Lenses" are made from a double layer of colored plastic wrap pasted to the tubes with rubber cement. When the students come to the library, they decorate their "binoculars" with magic markers and stickers. Then, donning plastic safari helmets (the kind used as favors for children's birthday parties), and with binoculars in hand, the students set out to find all the objects on their "Explore the Library" activity sheets. Included are such items as library catalog, magazines, computer, picture books, and pencil sharpener. When students have located all items, their list is checked. The adult checking the sheets asks each student to also point out at least three of the objects picked at random from the list.

— Sherry A. Kalbach, Cornwall (Pennsylvania) Elementary School

Keyword Help for Uncertain Spellers

Looking up books on the online catalog by keyword is a powerful tool but frustrating for elementary students who don't spell well. To help our students be more independent and to keep me from spelling the same words (e.g., *goosebumps, motorcycles, jokes, Arthur*) over and over again, I created "word books." For each circulation computer, I purchased an address book with alphabet tabs. I wrote the words students most frequently ask how to spell under the appropriate letter of the alphabet. Most children can figure out what letter a word starts with and then make the appropriate choice from the three to eight words they see on the page. Once they have the correct spelling, even kindergarten children can and do use keyword searching successfully.

— Lisa Delgado, South Jackson Elementary School, Athens, Georgia

Library ABCs

Almost every classroom has an alphabet hung high above the chalkboard. Why isn't there one in the library? We serve the same students who struggle with the alphabet in the classroom. I created our own Library ABCs. On nine- by 12-inch sheets of construction paper, I pasted a letter and a library word (e.g., *atlas, biography, catalog*).

— *Sherry A. Kalbach, Cornwall (Pennsylvania) Elementary School*

Ms. Book Demonstrates Book Care

Many years ago, for a graduate course, I made a large (16" x 24") book that showed by its torn, dirt-smeared, and fingerprinted pages how not to be a friend to a book. Although Ms. Book is now faded and yellowed, she is as popular with today's students as she was 20 years ago. I taped a 66-line rhyme that can be played as the book pages are shown. Often I choose to read the rhyme and talk about each misfortune as the children and I page through the book. Listeners discover that Ms. Book may start out sad due to mistreatment but "if you always take good care of her and treat her as your friend you'll find she has the biggest smile at the very end!"-

— *Sherry A. Kalbach, Cornwall (Pennsylvania) Elementary School*

Newbery Bingo

To familiarize students with Newbery titles, we play "Newbery Bingo" during the year. I use the paper dolls from the *American Girl* magazines and the trading cards from *Sports Illustrated for Kids* as prizes.

— *Joan Crawford, UMS-Wright Preparatory School, Mobile, Alabama*

Online & Hard Copy Searches

Frustrated by having only one online encyclopedia for a whole roomful of kids? To make this information more accessible, I bought a print version of *Grolier's Academic American Encyclopedia* for students to use in conjunction with the CD-ROM version. They first look up their topic on the computer using the keyword search. Then they browse through the articles until the find the ones they need. At that point, they turn the computer over to a waiting classmate and locate the identical article in the print encyclopedia. This method maximizes use of the CD-ROM version of the encyclopedia for searching and browsing and eliminates the need to use it for time-consuming studying and note taking. When you have one CD-ROM and 500 students who want to use it, this is the only way!

— *Jacque Burkhalter, Fidalgo Elementary School, Anacortes, Washington*

Paint Stirrers as Clues

To help children become independent library users, I use wooden paint-stirring sticks as clues to finding popular sections. I paint the wooden sticks in bright colors, affix a sticker representing topics such as dinosaurs, cars, fire fighters, and so forth. Then I write the general call number on the stick and coat the entire surface with permanent white glue. The sticks are kept in a decorated bucket. Children can look for the picture that represents their interest and then find the corresponding Dewey number. I've used these sticks for five years, and I've found that the children feel grown-up using them.

— *Pansy Fryman, Victor Ornelas Elementary, Garden City, Kansas*

Picture Cues at Circulation Stations

On the walls near the computer stations, I placed signs with pictures to help children spell the subjects they're looking up. For example, *dinosaur* would be printed out with a picture of a dinosaur on it. I used Print Shop software to make the signs. Children find the books they need quicker. This enables more students to use the stations.

— *Louise Warren, Beaverbrook Elementary School, Griffin, Georgia*

Recognizing the Screen

During our introduction and refresher sessions on the use of the computer catalog, we stress the importance of moving the screen back to its initial "Enter subject" setting when students or teachers leave the computer. This consistency allows even the youngest students to approach the catalog and know what their own first step needs to be.

— *Sharron L. McElmeel*

Ring of Good Books

When kindergartners and first graders select books, many go first to the "rings" hanging on pegboards in the picture book section. Laminated catalog cards feature pictures, clipped from catalogs, of popular easy titles with a call number in bold print for fiction or a computer graphic representing a subject such as dinosaurs with the Dewey number for nonfiction. Eight to 10 cards are grouped on each 1½-inch ring. Rings could be hung on cup racks or on pegboards.

— *Sally Ray, Wells Elementary School, Plano, Texas*

Shelving Nonfiction

To teach nonfiction book shelving, print out miscellaneous spine labels. Affix the labels to index cards or old shelf-list cards. Students can practice putting them in numerical order.

— *Ronda Nissen, Spring Bluff School, Winthrop Harbor, Illinois*

Something to Look Up

First and second grade students want to use the CD-ROM encyclopedia, but they usually do not have a topic or subject in mind. For readers, I create question cards, using the shaped notepapers found in stationery supply stores. Questions are written on the notepapers and laminated. Sample questions are "Can you find an illustration of a goldfish?" and "In which country is the official currency the yen?" For the nonreaders, I pasted a picture of an animal labeled with its name on a small square of paper. Students "draw" one of the cards and have a subject or a question to "look up." This allows them to be successful with an encyclopedia and a computer.

— *Iris T. Collins, Harrison Central Elementary School, Gulfport, Mississippi*

Storybook Trading Cards

To capitalize on student interest in card collecting, third grade students were asked to make "Storybook Trading Cards." The primary object of the lesson was to review the process of finding a book in the library. Students located one of their favorite books and completed the following information on a planning sheet: author, illustrator, title, call number, publisher, and copyright date. After looking at some commercially produced cards, students created a rough draft of a card for their selected book. Once the planning sheet was checked for accuracy, students took a piece of tagboard cut to the size of a trading card. On the front of the cards, they wrote the title and drew a picture relating to some scene or character from the book. On the back, they wrote the information necessary to locate a book in our library. Completed cards were inserted in the plastic sleeves designed to hold trading cards and these sleeves were kept in a notebook. The notebook serves as another source for students to use when they are looking for a book for recreational reading.

— *Bobbie Kuchta, Pedersen Elementary School, Altoona, Wisconsin*

Student-Made Dewey Posters

To reinforce learning the Dewey Decimal Classification System, I ask students to find pictures in magazines that show the classification subjects. The children are divided into groups of four and given scissors, glue, magic markers, poster board, and magazines. As they locate pictures they paste them on the board and label them with the Dewey numbers. I find that comprehension of the classification system improves after this activity.

— *Gelene Lineberger, Sherwood Elementary School, Gastonia, North Carolina*

Teeing Off for Library Skills

Students in grades 4-6 get hands-on practice in reference skills by playing golf without clubs. On flags shaped like those used on the golf course, print the names of things for students to look up, such as a word in a dictionary, a card in the catalog, a place on the globe, and Dewey numbers. Situate the flags around the library and give students numbered scorecards. The children check off the items as they progress from flag to flag. At the final flag or hole, children estimate the number of golf tees in a jar. The student whose estimation is the closest to the actual number wins a prize.

— *Diane Purdin, The King's Christian School, Haddon Heights, New Jersey*

Telephone Books Help Teach Indexing and Alphabetical Order

As part of an information skills lesson, we acquired a classroom set of telephone books from the local U.S. West office. The basic parts of the telephone book were introduced as we looked for information. Cooperative teams answered a series of questions.

— *Mary Childs, Park Rapids (Minnesota) Middle School*

The Stinky Cheese Man and Library Skills

Because Jon Scieszka and Lane Smith parodied every aspect of bookmaking in *The Stinky Cheese Man and Other Fairly Stupid Tales* (Viking, 1992), I use the book in explaining such bibliographic terms as *endpaper, title page, dedication page,* and *ISBN*. All are lampooned, making it easier for children to remember the terms and their meanings. The illustrations can also be used to teach typeface and text size since varying faces and sizes are used.

— *Andrea Troisi, LaSalle Middle School, Niagara Falls, New York*

SECTION 5

Managing the Library

> ## Lots of folks confuse bad management with destiny.
>
> *Kim Hubbard*

Management of the library is the job that few others will notice unless the management is poor then—they will notice. It is also the part of your job that is probably least appreciated as most of your peers will not realize all that goes into the efforts to keep the library media center and its materials accessible to them and their students. The experience and suggestions of others may provide you with some ideas you can use to make your management of the center easier. Our next section will provide suggestions for letting others know just what you do accomplish in the library media center.

MARC Tag—659

The Accelerated Reader (AR) program has increased the use of the media center materials at our school. Since our media center's electronic catalog is networked school-wide, it was important to indicate which books were AR books on the database. This was accomplished by using the 659 tag in the MARC (Machine Readable Cataloging) record of each AR book. When a patron does a subject search using the keywords "Accelerated Reader" a list of all the titles will appear for the patron to scan through in order to see what is checked in and checked out of the media center. The category feature can be utilized in order to print out a list of the books purchased for the AR program and their circulation statistics. This will enable the media specialist to show use of the books and possibly obtain more from the budget to support the program.

— *Katherine M. Smith, Columbus, Georgia*

A Poem for a Magazine

To control the gatherings at the magazine rack during class book exchanges, I require students to memorize a poem for "magazine privileges." Copies of a short poem with a book or library theme are available for those who want to try. Students are given one chance a week to recite the poem.

— *Ronda Nissen, Spring Bluff School, Winthrop Harbor, Illinois*

Adopt a Shelf

In past years, student library helpers often lost their enthusiasm for the job before the year was over. This year we initiated an "adopt-a-shelf" program. Each student-volunteer is assigned a section of shelves. He is responsible for keeping the books tidy and in order. Now, the volunteers come to the library every day and are protective of their designated shelf. The volunteers will get adoption papers (certificates) at the end of the year. The library has never looked better.

— *Lee C. Basye, Winston Park Elementary School, Miami, Florida*

Another Use for Gift Bags

I use gift bags stuffed with tissue paper to identify sections of the book collection for kindergarten and first grade children. For example, a gift bag with pictures of dogs identifies the 600s; one with dinosaurs, the 500s, and another with sports scenes, the 700s. The bags are an inexpensive way to make the library more attractive and user friendly.

— *Linda Nichols, Cain Elementary, Whitehouse, Texas*

Another Use for Shelf Markers

I use plastic shelf markers to teach first graders location skills. On one side of a marker, I write a letter of the alphabet for the fiction shelves. On the other side, I write a number found in the nonfiction section. The children select markers and then locate a book from the sections indicated. Large colorful letters and numbers are placed on the walls above the shelves. To explain the organization of the fiction sections, I ask the children to pretend that they are authors and go to the shelf where their books would be shelved.

— *Linda Nichols, Cain Elementary, Whitehouse, Texas*

Authors' Photos on Walls and Shelves

Following several author visits, I hung framed photos of the authors under a banner reading "Authors We Have Known." The display created so much attention that we put other photos that were taken at state conferences in acrylic frames and set them on the shelves near the authors' books. On the fiction shelves, in the "S" section there's a photo of William Sleator; in the 811s students find a photo of Jack Prelutsky.

— *Wendy Braddock, Indian Hill Middle School, Cincinnati, Ohio*

B & B in the Library

No, not bed and breakfast—breakfast and books! We had an office full of new books when we returned to school in August. Instead of a formal session for teachers on new literature, we invited them to breakfast in the library between 7:30 and 9:30. We had a big pot of coffee, a jug of orange juice, lots of "munchies," and new books spread out on the tables. We didn't wait until all the books were processed. We just put them on the tables in all stages of being processed. Self-adhesive notes were available so teachers could put their names on books they wanted to check out as soon as the books were ready. We found this to be successful way to stir up excitement about reading.

— *Sue McGown, Lower School Library, St. John's School, Houston, Texas*

Baby Wipes

We have found that baby wipes work great in a library. We use them to clean dirty books, or especially dirty little hands. They're also great for cleaning the tables.

— *Gail Wood, East Side Elementary, Magnolia, Arkansas*

Barcode Everything

Barcode and check out everything that can be taken out the door. When the item comes up on the overdue list, you'll know where to find it. Any flat surface can be barcoded (e.g., CDROM caddies, calculators, rulers, three-hole punches). Attach shop tags with barcodes to equipment and make a book card with the same barcode (to be used in tracking the equipment). If equipment is sent out for repair, check it out for four weeks to a patron named REPAIR. Write the name of the service company on the card kept for tracking. If the item comes up overdue, it's time to call and inquire about the repair delay. If an item cannot be barcoded (e.g., scissors, protractor, compass, magnifying glass), check it out as a temporary item. Use a clear catalog card protector or recipe card saver over a bar-coded book card. Identify the item on a two- by four -inch "form" under the protector, leaving the barcode showing above it. Barcoded cards in protectors can be kept ready for use at the circulation desk, and patrons can fill out special forms before checking out items such as vertical files. Temporary barcode cards, protectors, and forms in use can be filed in the charge tray like book cards. Equipment cards may also be stored in the old charge tray for quick tracking of equipment

— *Janet Hofstetter, California (Missouri) High School*

Barcodes & Business Cards

I keep the children's barcoded library cards in a business card holder that accommodates 10 cards per page. I write a child's name on both sides of a card and put the barcode on the plastic cover. The cards are filed by classroom, and there are no lost cards.

— Rebecca Easley, Hattie Watts Elementary School, Patterson, Louisiana

Barcodes in Coffee Cans

When we automated, we made a barcode card for each child. We filed the cards by class in the small oblong cans in which flavored coffees are sold. The cans were covered with contact sheets. When children come to the library independently, they get their barcode card from the class can, use it to check out books, and return the card behind the letter divider. No lost or wrinkled cards! Next year we will have students retrieve their cards from the year before and file them in their new class cans. This will save us time because we won't have to make new cards for returning students or sort and re-file the cards ourselves.

— Pat Miller, Walker Station Elementary School, Sugar Land, Texas

Barcoding CDs

At our school, we catalog and barcode each compact disc that circulates. The barcode is attached to the CD's case. We use a permanent-ink marking pen to write the barcode number on the top of the disc so we can identify the copy if a disc is separated from its case.

— Sharron L. McElmeel

Book Fair Workers

Twice a year, our library sponsors a book fair. For the past several years, we have asked retired teachers to come in and staff the sales table for us. I put a sign in the teacher's lounge with all the names of the retired teachers who will be working during the book fair. Teachers stop in to say hello to old friends and colleagues, and often buy a book, too. Most of these retired teachers are grandparents, and they love to buy books for their grandchildren. They have been some of our best customers, as well as great workers!

— Karen Hildebrand, Willis Middle School, Delaware, Ohio

Book Swap

Since we close the library for checkouts two weeks before school is out, our library sponsored a Book Swap—a recycling day for books. Students received a coupon for each paperback book they brought to trade. During the final check out, they could pick out paperbacks and pay with coupons. Even the teachers joined in. Any books that were not "bought" with coupons were given to charity.

— *Becky Menti, Starrett Elementary School, Arlington, Texas*

Books for Parents

Take advantage of the automated circulation system by including the names of parents in the database. Not only is this practice good for public relations, but it also encourages parents to select books for reading at home. I find that the most frequent users of this service are parents of nursery and kindergarten children.

— *Leah G. McIlvain, Model Laboratory School, Eastern Kentucky University, Richmond, Kentucky*

[Editor's Note: This hint will help to encourage parents and even grandparents to visit the library media center with their children, whether school-aged or preschool-aged. During kindergarten round-up sessions each spring, hand out a brief list of books adults may wish to share with their children, and extend a sincere invitation for them to bring their incoming kindergartner to the center anytime during the day. When they come enter the child's name in the computer, give each child his or her checkout number, and give the visitors a tour of the library. If the child comes back during a literature time when a primary class is in the library media center invite the child to sit with the class and listen to the story. The positive public relations the school will receive for these gestures will be astounding—and in the process you will encourage another family to read together.]

Books on Wheels

When one of four libraries I administer was being rebuilt, the books sat in inaccessible storage. To keep the children's love of reading and the library alive, I selected books for all grade levels from the other school libraries and the public library. I set up a flexible once-a-week schedule with each teacher and spent my day at the "under-renovation school" going from classroom to classroom reading aloud. For K-grade 3, I selected books that could be read in 15 to 20 minutes. I also tried to include new books that would be found in the school when the library reopened. Fourth and fifth graders enjoyed two of the books that were nominees for the state's children's book award. I read the two books to them a few chapters at a time. A travel bag on wheels was a lifesaver for lugging eight to 10 books and a planning notebook through the hallways. I ended those days of reading aloud tired and hoarse, but sharing books with an appreciative audience made it all worthwhile. It also sustained excitement for the midyear opening of the new library.

— *Catherine Andronik, Seymour (Connecticut) Public Schools*

Bull's-Eye for No Overdues

To encourage students to return books in time for inventory, I hang a large bull's-eye target outside the library during the last two weeks of school. Each class is represented by an arrow. Part of the arrowhead is missing, so it appears that the arrow has penetrated the target. As students turn in books, their class arrow is moved closer to the center. The color of the feathers indicates the grade level and the teachers' names are written on the shaft so students can follow their class's progress. The outer ring represents more than six books out, and the inner rings count down by 6 to 5, 4 to 3, 2 to 1, and finally "All Books Returned!" Recently, I have begun rewarding classes that have returned or paid for all of their books by holding a drawing for two to four books as prizes.

— *Lisa J. Delgado, South Jackson Elementary School, Athens, Georgia*

Target for the Barcode Reader

Many hands use the expensive barcode reader with our automated program, so we want to protect it. We made a pad from some sheets of blue packing foam. The bright color gives volunteers a target each time they put the reader on the counter.

— *Pat Miller, Walker Station Elementary School, Sugar Land, Texas*

Cards on a Ring

For our automated check-out system, the children's library cards are organized by classes and hung on a ring. The teacher's name is on the top card. Each grade level has a different color for the teacher's card. When an entire class comes to the library, I take cards off the ring and place them on a table. The students find their card, check out a book, and file their cards by their last name in an organizer file. After the class leaves, I remove the cards from the organizer and put them back on the ring.

— *Marynel Adams, Lucille Moore Elementary School, Panama City, Florida*

Cataloging Magazines

I catalog issues of Cobblestone, Calliope, Faces, and Odyssey magazines into my Winnebago circulation/catalog system so students and teachers can quickly search the subject headings of these valuable publications.

— *Wayne Rush, Grover Cleveland Middle School, Caldwell, New Jersey*

Chart for Sharing Nonprint Materials

Prior to the first of each month, I pull all films, videos, and audiocassettes that feature a holiday or special observance occurring in that month. Teachers are given a sign-up schedule for the month, which allows them to reserve the material for a showing in the classroom or in the media center. This has resulted in a tenfold increase in the use of these time-specific materials.

— *Owen Ditchfield, Edward A. White Elementary School, Fort Benning, Georgia*

Checkouts at a Glance

I use a "visual" check-out system in our primary school library (K-grade 3). For each class I make charts using poster board and low-back pockets. Students' names are written on labels and attached to the pockets. Their "library cards" are three- by five-inch index cards with the teacher's initials and the student's name written on them. When the student checks out a book, he or she simply trades cards with me. The book card goes in the chart pocket; the student's card goes in the book. When classes come to the library, we can quickly check in books by trading cards. With a glance at the poster, I can see who has overdue books.

— *Joni Cain, Sutter Creek Primary School, Jackson, California*

[Editor's Note: With the automation of library media centers, there are, of course, no more book cards to trade in this manner. However, the basic idea can serve many purposes. For example, in schools with flexible schedule and check-out times, a chart in classrooms with a "library card" in each child's pocket can visually let the teacher know whether or not the child has visited the library during that particular week. At the beginning of the week "library cards" go into each child's pocket. When the child comes to the library for the FIRST time during a week, he selects the library card from his pocket and transfers it to the a nearby basket. On the last day of the week, the teacher will send all the children who still have a library card in their pocket to the library media center. This ensures that each child visits the library at least once during the week. The automated check-out system will show the status of each child's books and will provide an opportunity to discuss any overdue book situation with the child.]

Checking Internet Use Permission

We created a procedure that helps us fulfill our school board's requirement that students have parent permission to use e-mail and the Internet. We give each student a single sheet with the full text of the Acceptable Use Policy on one side and a form for parents, students, and the building principal to sign on the other side. We put the sheets in a file and compile a computerized list for ready reference. We ask that students display their school picture ID cards near the keyboard every time they log on. We can easily check the ID against our alphabetized parent permission list.

— *Edna Boardman, Minot (North Dakota) High School, Magic City Campus*

Christmas in August

At the beginning of the school year I was faced with a large backlog of unprocessed books and software. To ensure that I would be processing the items most needed first, I held a "Christmas party" in August during school planning week. When the teachers arrived in the media center, they were greeted with holiday music, hot cider and doughnuts, and the "presents" (the new materials) covering every available table and low bookshelf top. At each spot where there was a set of books, a collection of videos, or other grouping of materials, there was a three- by five-inch index card with the name of the items. Each teacher had been provided with a supply of gummed stars to use for votes. By putting one or more of their stars on the index card for each grouping of items, the teachers could indicate what things they needed most. To wrap up the day, we had drawings for door prizes.

— *Owen Ditchfield, Edward A. White School, Fort Benning, Georgia*

Class Barcodes by Color

Student barcodes in our circulation system are organized by homeroom and kept in a notebook on the circulation desk. When you open the notebook to any class, all class members' cards are visible. The barcodes are mounted on 1½" x 3" cards that can be fed through a dot matrix computer. Cards are taped to construction paper cut to fit inside plastic sleeves, which can be scanned. Each grade has been assigned a different color, so even kindergarten students can quickly find their class. At the beginning of each school year, I just slit the tape with a sharp knife and rearrange the cards by the new classroom rolls.

— *Lisa Delgado, South Jackson Elementary School, Athens, Georgia*

Clipboard Organization

When I have several ongoing projects, I use what I call the "clipboard lineup." In the library office I hang clipboards for each of the projects I'm working on. I hang them with the backs facing out and label them with the project name. It's an easy way to keep organized. Just grab the clipboard and make notes.

— *Patricia Kolencik, North Clarion High School, Tionesta, Pennsylvania*

Clipboards

We purchased 30 clipboards and placed them in racks by the main door to the media center. Students use them to keep papers and search strategy forms organized and as a writing surface at stand-up or crowded search stations.

— *Mary Alice Anderson, Winona (Minnesota) Middle School*

Collectible Library Furnishings

With the "mission style" popular in home decorating now, library furnishings and supplies are suddenly fashionable. People are snapping up traditional oak library tables and slat-back chairs to convert into dining room furniture. Wood charging trays and stacking trays are turned into the latest look in closet organizers. Card catalog cabinets are in big demand by baseball card collectors, who have found the drawer system perfect for organizing collections. Some card catalogs are being resurrected as coffee tables and end tables. Now that America has discovered the classic styling of library furnishings, you can turn your discards into cash for the library.

— *Andrea Troisi, LaSalle Middle School, Niagara Falls, New York*

Color-Coding Books

Since the library serves more than 1,000 students in K-grade 7, we don't always have time to go to the shelves with students. We have found that color-coding the frequently needed books helps young children make their own selections. We put orange dots on the spines of the "easy" books to show that they are appropriate for kindergarten children. On the fiction shelves, books nominated for the state book awards have a blue dot. Beginning chapter books for early primary students have green dots. In the general collection, we use red dots for multicultural titles. When a student wants or needs a particular type of book, the book can easily be located by the colors.

— *Donna Boling, Avondale Elementary, Decatur, Georgia*

Coming Prepared

During the first few months after our computer catalog was installed, the question most asked was "How do you spell...?" Invariably the question had to be answered more than once as the student laboriously wrote down the spelling. Yes, the computer would get close to the selection if the word was misspelled, but it wasn't close enough for some youngsters. Now, during computer catalog instruction, we emphasize that the youngsters should come prepared with the subjects, authors, or titles that they wish to look up, written on a piece of paper. Even the youngest students have more success with their searches.

— *Sharron L. McElmeel*

Cordless Freedom

Until recently, we relied on lung power to relay information to those servicing our workstations. One staff member would hold the office phone and relay the advice offered by the customer support rep at the other end. It was a frustrating and noisy situation. Our problem was solved when we bought a cordless phone. It has given us incredible freedom to move around and fix things while talking to technical support people. We also carry the phone with us when we check the shelves for book requests phoned in by teachers, administrators and other libraries.

— *Joyce Valenza, Wissahickon High School, Ambler, Pennsylvania*

Dewey Who?

Children in our elementary school (K-grade 3) often want to use the nonfiction sections, but many are unable to read the headings in the card catalog. To help them, I created a "Knock! Knock" folder. On the front of a colorful file folder I drew a doorknob and key plate to resemble a door and wrote in cartoon balloons the phrases "Who's there?"; "Dewey!"; "Dewey Who?" Inside I pasted pictures of the animals and objects the children most frequently want books about (horses, dogs, sports, space, and dinosaurs) and labeled them with the Dewey number. The folder is laminated. It has been well used.

— *Iris T. Collins, Harrison Central Elementary School, Gulfport, Mississippi*

Doing the "Five in Five"

Can't get your books put away? When books start piling up, I do a "five in five" with a few of my intermediate classes. As students are arriving, I use the first five minutes to have each student put five books on top of the bookshelf where they belong. Each section of shelves is labeled for quick checking. Students have a series of lessons on book location skills prior to assisting with "five in five." Library volunteers then put the books away on the shelves. The job goes much quicker, and the books are correctly re-shelved.

— *Jacque Burkhalter, Fidalgo Elementary School, Anacortes, Washington*

Drive That Winnebago!

I use an external hard drive as a backup for my Winnebago software system for the Macintosh. At the end of each day, I just drag my system folder to my external hard drive icon to copy. It copies everything in just a few minutes. When I need to catch up on time-consuming projects such as adding new patrons or cataloging in new materials, I disconnect the external hard drive, take it home, and hook it up to my own Macintosh. Then I open up my Winnebago circulation/catalog program and get to work. When I return to school, I copy my Winnebago system folder to the drive in my main computer.

— *Wayne Rush, Grover Cleveland Middle School, Caldwell, New Jersey*

Easy-to-Find Procedures

If you subscribe to database services such as Wilson or Dialog, make cards for common procedures and for online emergency procedures. Make a separate card for each popular file on a database, listing appropriate commands and formats from the service's manual (such as from Dialog's blue sheets). Post basic procedures for database services on a bulletin board that is visible from the computer used for accessing the service.

— *Janet Hofstetter, California (Missouri) High School*

Equipment Records on the Automated Circulation System

An automated circulation/inventory system is a great timesaver for keeping track of equipment. We enter all computers and other equipment in the database, along with each item's purchase order number, purchase date, price, and the business office's identifying number. We use the "message" feature of the system to record repairs and maintenance. This information is invaluable when it's time to check warranties, make insurance claims, or decide if equipment should be repaired or replaced.

— *Mary Alice Anderson, Winona (Minnesota) Middle School*

Free Resource for Librarians

The Librarian's Yellow Pages is an all-advertising directory organized in an easy-to-use yellow pages format. This resource lists all the sources you can imagine for acquiring library "stuff." To receive a free copy, request one online at <http://www.LibrariansYellowPages.com/>. The online version of this useful database is searchable by keyword or company name and is updated monthly.

— *Jacque Burkhalter, Fidalgo Elementary School, Anacortes, Washington*

From Paper to Electronic Catalogs with Help

When you are switching from a paper card catalog to an electronic catalog (and doing the job yourself), enlist the help of the teachers and students. Ask the students to pull shelf cards, assign barcode numbers, and box up books in the same subject areas. The teachers and students can enter the records at network computers. A contest with progress notes on bar graphs will maintain interest in the project.

— *Eleanor S. Bayles, Grenville Christian College, Brockville, Ontario, Canada*

Good Memories for Barcodes

Since we use a flexible schedule, children do not come to the library as a class group. Rather than keeping a print record of barcode numbers, we ask children to memorize their numbers. We found that even preschoolers were able to memorize a three-digit number. The process is made easier because children have the same number for the automated school lunch system. Of course, there's always a record in the computer at the check-out desk should a child forget.

— *Sharron L. McElmeel*

Home Connections to Reading

During the final library class of the school year, my students recycled old neckties into bookworms. Early in the year I asked parents to donate men's wide neckties—this provided the nearly 600 ties needed for the school-wide project. In addition to the ties, we needed just a few simple supplies, including scissors, glue, scrap paper or newspaper for stuffing, scraps of construction paper or felt, and ribbon for the neck bow. I provided buttons, sequins, and other odds and ends for the extra touches, such as fancy eyes, that the student might want to add. To make the bookworms, lightly crumple scrap paper and stuff it loosely as far down inside the tie as possible. The wide point of the tie front becomes the head and also should be stuffed. Eyes, lashes, tongue, nostrils, and other features are cut from paper or felt. A ribbon tied around the neck adds the finishing touch. The children take their bookworms home. I suggest they use them to decorate bookshelves, headboards or curtain rods as reminders to read throughout the summer vacation.

— *Sherry A. Kalbach, Cornwall (Pennsylvania) Elementary School*

Ideas in the Bank

As Director of Library Services for the schools in a diocese, I ask the librarians in the schools to "deposit" their good ideas and helpful hints in my "Idea Bank." I share the ideas with all librarians, but especially with those who are new to the diocese.

— *Barbara Chatam, Diocese of Galveston-Houston, Texas*

Identifying Discards as You Go

Throughout the year, I come across books that are outdated or need to be replaced. But, at the end of the year, I cannot remember which ones. My solution: I entered the subject headings "Discards (Outdated) June (year)" and "Discards (Worn or Damaged) June (year)" in the automated circulation system. During the year, it takes only minutes to pull up a book title and click in the "discard" subject heading. At the end of the year, I print a list of all books with the "discard" heading. The same system works for nonprint items.

— *Juanita I. Brown, Franklin County High School, Carnesville, Georgia*

Identifying Software Disks

Put an identifying label, such as the American Library Association's library logo, on floppy disks that belong to the media center. Use color-coding (either stickers or different color disk labels) to differentiate among various kinds of software—games, databases, and tutorials.

— *Patricia Burns, Crary Middle School, Waterford, Michigan*

Index Cards Find a Place in Automated Systems

Often our youngest students, and even older ones, get sidetracked in the library and forget to check out their books. We have an automated circulation system, but we don't have a security system. Yellow index cards are our solution. As students check out books at the computer station, they slip a yellow index card in the book pocket. When the class leaves the library, we ask students to show us the yellow card in their books. We can tell at a glance who forgot. When a new student's name is not in the computer, we fill out a temporary book card and insert a green card in his library book. When the book is returned, the green card alerts us to add the student's name.

— *Pat Miller, Walker Station Elementary, Sugar Land, Texas*

Installing Patron Station

If you are just now automating or have automated the library's catalog and still have reluctant users who are clinging to the old card catalog, you might be interested in how I solved the problem. I installed one patron station on a separate switch, loading a backup copy of data, and setting it to automatically boot up to the search function when the computer is turned on. An easy-to-follow set of directions for search, browse, and print functions accompanies the station, which is used after hours. Every few weeks I update the backup data so that it reflects the library's most current holdings. A clipboard for staff to request materials is kept at the station, and my aide and I check this each morning, tracking down items as needed. For sure-fire impact, you could install this station in the same location as that occupied by your old card catalog. What a surprise for those technophobes on your staff!

— *Jacque Burkhalter, Fidalgo Elementary School Anacortes, Washington*

Keeping Posters on the Walls

Have trouble with posters sliding down the wall if they've been attached with masking tape "rolls" on the back? I've discovered that placing the "rolls" at 90-degree angles to each other in the top and bottom corner of the poster may be the answer. Since the tape rolls are going in opposite directions, the force of gravity doesn't pull the posters down as easily.

— *Carol Burbridge, Jardine Middle School, Topeka, Kansas*

Keeping Students On-Task with Color-Coding

The popularity of electronic encyclopedias, atlases, and the Internet have created unique supervision issues for practicing media specialists. I have devised a system of colored badges for each electronic resource in my media center. Students pick up these colored badges from the circulation desk to show what resource they will be using. The use of bright fluorescent colors (pink for Internet, green for multimedia encyclopedias, and so forth) has helped me to determine if students are staying on-task and using the resource appropriately. I can see these brightly colored badges easily from across the media center. The responsibility of supervising students has become less time-consuming, as well as result-oriented.

— *Jill Davidson, Eagle's Landing Middle School, McDonough, Georgia*

Keeping Tabs on Read-Alouds

Here is an organized way to keep track of the books you have read aloud to classes. Keep a small recipe box with index cards on your desk. For each read-aloud book, write the title and author's name on a card. After each story hour or booktalk, write down the date, teacher's name and grade level for the book you featured. This alphabetical file will serve as a reminder to you and avoid repetition for the children.

— *Doris M. Baker, Urbin T. Kelley/Plantsville Elementary Schools, Shelton, Connecticut*

Keeping Video Items Up-to-Date

Allow teachers to help you keep the video collection up-to-date and current. Devise a simple checklist so teachers can alert you regarding a video's relevancy to the curriculum. With each video checked out to a teacher, attach the following form:

Was the video current?	Yes ☐	No ☐
Was it useful?	Yes ☐	No ☐
Would you recommend it?	Yes ☐	No ☐

When the video is returned, the form is expected to be with it. If a video is not current, consider discarding it.

— *Barbara Abernathy, Bremen, Georgia*

Kitchen Timers

How many times have you wanted to videotape something from the satellite or cable on different tapes but forgot to switch tapes? I set a kitchen timer to ring a couple of minutes before I should switch the tapes. I also use the timer when a teacher sends a student to read in the media center for 15 minutes. When the timer goes off, I send the student back to class.

— *Kimberly M. Casleton, South Columbus Elementary School, Columbus, Georgia*

Labeled Lamps

When you store new boxes of projector lamps, write the name of the equipment on the boxes. Next time you reach for a lamp in the supply cupboard, you won't have to search your memory to recall which lamp fits which projector.

— *Judie Weiss, Waples Mill School, Oakton, Virginia*

Labels for the Shelves

Label your shelves like a grid: Column A, Column B, and so forth across the top; and Row 1, Row 2, Row 3, and so on down the side. When kids ask, "Where are the pet books?" you can say, "636, Row 1 Column F." Students become familiar with graphs while they are using the library, and everyone saves time.

— *Ronda Nissen, Spring Bluff School, Winthrop Harbor, Illinois*

Learn from Your Colleagues' Errors

You can make barcodes quickly and easily with your printer. In the days when most of us used dot matrix printers we had to worry about changing the print ribbon often. If we did not, we ended up labeling many books with barcodes too pale to be read by our scanner. Now with many of us using laser-like printers, such as DeskWriters, we must be careful that our print function specifies the best quality. Our advice: If in doubt, try it out.

— *Mary Hauge, West High School, Aurora, Illinois*

Library Club

We have a library club for fourth and fifth graders who like to help in the media center. Students who participate are required to give up one day of recess per week and help with shelving, dusting, errands, and other tasks. The club members get their picture in the school yearbook and receive a free book from the book fair, a certificate on awards day, and a small treat on holidays.

— *Margie Hall, Chapel Hill Elementary, Douglasville, Georgia*

Library Job Application

In our K-grade 5 school, fifth graders may "apply" to work one recess period per week in the media center. Because the work they do is so needed in a library serving 22 classes and 22 teachers, we require these volunteers to fill out an application form. They must give two references and have the signatures of a parent and a classroom teacher. Those applying go through a training program and take an oral exam. Students are expected to meet their work schedule and be on time. They can be "let go" for missing work or not doing their work but those who stay on provide a valuable service to the school.

— *Janice Hampton, Jeffries Elementary School, Springfield, Missouri*

Listening Center Helps to Recycle Card Catalog

We store audiotape cassettes in the drawers of the old card catalog. The catalog's legs have been cut down to five inches in height. On top of the catalog we placed a cassette player with headsets, a few books with tapes, and a stuffed animal. A child can select a tape from a drawer, sit down in a rocking chair nearby, and listen to a tape before checking it out.

— *Judith Weiss & Pat Mudrick, Waples Mill Elementary School, Oakton, Virginia*

Liven Up the Look of Computer Monitors

Liven up dull, gray computer monitors with handmade "screenies"-computer screen frames of heavy-duty laminated cardboard that measure 16 inches by 131/4 inches to fit 13-inch, 14-inch, and 15-inch monitors. The "screenies" are easy to mount with Velcro. Make them out of gift-wrap for special occasions or decorate them with clip art. Have students make their own personalized "screenies" using blank frames experimenting with fanciful shapes. A brontosaurus shape, for example, could have an area in its center to accommodate the screen of the monitor.

— *Andrea Troisi, LaSalle Middle School, Niagara Falls, New York*

Manage Your Mail

A simple system of file folders can help you manage floods of incoming mail and keep your desk tidy, too! Label five folders by days of the workweek; label the sixth one "next week." As mail arrives, put it into the appropriate folder and tag urgent items. When you've finished, put five of the files aside so you can concentrate on the current day's folder at an uncluttered desk.

— *Sandy Nelson, Lee County Schools, Fort Myers, Florida*

Managing Circulation Cards

For an easy and efficient way to manage circulation cards in an elementary school library, buy a three-ring binder approximately three inches wide, a pack of slide protectors, and poster board in a different color for each of the grades in your school. Cut the poster board into 2-inch squares to fit into each slide holder. After assigning barcodes on the automated system, place the barcode and the name of each student on a two-inch square card. Label one or two protector sheets for each teacher in your school. Arrange barcoded squares alphabetically in the slide protectors by class roll. Place the binder on the circulation desk where it is available for each patron or class that visits the media center. No more lost cards, frustrated teachers, or re-made checkout cards. At the beginning of the next year, simply update the computer and rearrange students in their new classes. Delete the graduating class and assign those barcode numbers to the incoming group. You never have to make cards again!

— *Vicki Bland, North Fayette Elementary School, Morrow, Georgia*

Marking the Spot

Inexpensive plastic rulers are good shelf markers. They're easy to replace if they are broken or lost. Just keep a supply at the circulation desk for children to pick up before they browse the shelves.

— *Phyllis Breuer, Spalding University, Louisville, Kentucky*

Minimizing the Waste Time

Reassess what you are doing with your time and set priorities.

▶ Don't do unnecessary work. Automation has eliminated many labor-intensive tasks (e.g., typing and updating bibliographies or overdue lists). When deciding what tasks to eliminate, ask yourself: Does it make a difference to the learner? Can someone else do it?

▶ Write down ideas before you forget them. Better yet, keep your ideas and "to-do" lists on your computer.

▶ Computerize anything that can be! Use spreadsheets and databases to keep track of things such as equipment and supply bids and quotes, budgets, program statistics, warranty and repair information, software costs, and orders. Update these files often so record keeping does not become an overwhelming task.

▶ Develop templates for letters and reports.

▶ Ask vendors to provide written price information when you are ordering quantities of supplies. This saves you the time of looking through catalogs or making phone calls.

- ▶ Develop good relationships with vendors so you can rely on them for help and information.
- ▶ Use your automation system to keep track of anything and everything that circulates. When possible, customize records to enable students to locate resources independently.
- ▶ Try to limit book purchases to vendors who supply electronic cataloging records. When electronic records cannot be purchased, copy cataloging from another electronic catalog such as the one at the public library or local university.
- ▶ Record purchase order, warranty, price, and serial number information for all capital items in your automation system. This information is invaluable in case of theft or repair under warranty.
- ▶ To the extent that is possible, have the same software and utilities on all computers.
- ▶ Use your old card catalog for storing bulbs, batteries, cables, and other small supply items. Keep these items in alphabetical order.
- ▶ Be selective in regard to what mail you actually open and read.
- ▶ Keep file cabinets manageable by throwing something away each time you file. Cut down on what you need to file by keeping your own information in electronic format. Discard outdated technology information.
- ▶ Use telephones, faxes, and e-mail for correspondence when possible.
- ▶ Keep important paperwork and manuals on a given item, including the network, in one place.
- ▶ Weed materials in all formats continuously and constantly. Weeding is not a huge task if you pull materials as you come across them.
- ▶ Develop the habit of making good decisions quickly. Rapid changes in technology require that you not wait for something better to come along.
- ▶ Just do it!

— *Mary Alice Anderson, Winona (Minnesota) Middle School*

New Uses for Old Tennis Balls

Dragging chair legs across the tile floor made the computer lab noisy. The principal got old tennis balls from a tennis club, cut them open and stuck them on the chair legs. After that, it was remarkably quiet.

— *Kathy Gough, Schneider Elementary School, North Aurora, Illinois*

On-Hold and Busy

Two of our best purchases last year were a large computer monitor and a portable phone. The monitor is wonderful when we are creating Web pages. The portable phone is especially helpful during long "on-hold" waits for customer support. We can move to the ailing computer when someone comes on the line. While waiting, we can go on with regular media center activities.

— *Mary Alice Anderson, Winona (Minnesota) Middle School*

Organizing Icons & CD-ROMs

Because we now have more than 50 CD-ROMs on our network, the menu was becoming unmanageable and confusing for students. To improve organization, our Windows Program Manager icons now appear under a Dewey number plus a verbal heading. For example, accessing 800-899 Literature brings up *Disc/It* and *Discovering Authors*. We also offer word processing programs and other CD-ROMs under separate icons. This has made a real difference in student access.

— *Jacqueline Seewald, Red Bank Regional High School, Little Silver, New Jersey*

Pen on a Rope

I was always misplacing my pen until I got a "pen on a rope," which I wear around my neck every day. Now I always have a pen handy.

— *Meg Miranda, Highland View Middle School, Corvallis, Oregon*

"Please Stand on the Snowflakes"

It is sometimes difficult for young children to understand the directions "stand in a straight line." I try to help them by providing a "line" for them to stand on. I simply cut out shapes—different ones for different times of the year (leaves for fall, snowflakes for winter, hearts for Valentine's Day, and flowers for spring)—then paste them to square pieces of paper, laminate, and tape them to the carpet with heavy-duty, clear packaging tape. I place the squares in a line in front of the circulation desk, leaving approximately one foot of space between each shape. Instead of constantly saying, "stand in a straight line," I simply ask the children to stand on a leaf, snowflake, flower, and so on. It's fun for them and it works great for me!

— *Donna Boling, Avondale Elementary School, DeKalb County Schools, Decatur, Georgia*

Practical Reasons to Tape

Videotape the lecture and demonstration portions of any workshops you conduct. You can use the tape later to review your presentation and to present information to new teachers or those who did not attend.

— *Sandy Pope, South Elementary School, Eldon, Missouri*

Pre-Printed Entries

Before going to conferences, print out some mailing labels with your name, school, and address. It will be a cinch to enter the many drawings or sign up for mailing lists.

— *Ronda Nissen, Spring Bluff School, Winthrop Harbor, Illinois*

Principal for a Day

We use one of the computer-based reading comprehension programs. Students earn points when they successfully pass computer-generated tests on books they have read. We allow students to buy items at the library store when they have accumulated a number of points. This was expensive until I came up with certificates that could be "sold." On our computer we made certificates that entitled students to be a principal, assistant principal, or coach for a day. The students bought the positions with their reading points. All students are now asking how many points they need to buy one of these positions. The secretaries and the counselor have asked that we include certificates for their positions. I also sell a certificate to have lunch in the library with the principal.

— *Pam Wingate, Rayburn Elementary School, McAllen, Texas*

Putting the Place in Order-Inventory Ideas

By the end of the year, the picture books are usually a jumble, even if they are shelved alphabetically. This makes conducting an inventory a nightmare. As a fast way to get the books inventoried, I enlist the help of each scheduled library class. I remove all books in the "A" section and distribute them at the rate of four to six books per student in the first class. I ask the students to pile the books in front of them so they can see the titles. Then I call off the titles from the accession drawer for picture books. The student who has this book puts it on the shelf. If no one can find the "called" book, I put a paper clip on the accession card. You can make a game of this activity to reward the student helpers. And, children are given a chance to look at books they might not otherwise seek out.

— *Andrea Troisi, LaSalle Middle School, Niagara Falls, New York*

[Editor's Note: Even if you inventory via your computer system don't overlook this procedure for straightening the shelves at the end of the school year—to provide an "orderly" beginning the following school year.]

Puzzle Table

Don't throw away your children's old board and box puzzles. Ask teachers and parents to donate puzzles. The puzzle table in our library is the most popular attraction during free time. Puzzles appeal to all ages, too.

— *Pam Whitehead, Tishomingo (Mississippi) Elementary School*

Recycled Disks

We recycle old computer disks as computer passes. The homeroom teachers write their names on the disks. When a student comes to the media center with the disk, we know that he has permission from the teacher to use the computer. Earlier we had a problem with students who were sent to the center to check out books and instead went to the computer.

— *Belinda Thompson, Berta Weathersbee Elementary School, LaGrange, Georgia*

Recycling Laminating Film

A teacher in our school recycles the scraps of plastic from laminating projects as film for transparencies. She cuts the scraps into page-size rectangles and uses water-based, overhead-projection pens to write on them. Students can wash the ink from the film and use it over and over again for their presentations. This saves our school the cost of write-on transparency sheets.

— *Phyllis Press, Manchester Township Middle School, Lakehurst, New Jersey*

Reference Cards Simplify Cataloging

When cataloging and entering information about MARC tags, fixed-field codes, and user-defined categories, I found it cumbersome to refer to manuals and difficult to rely on my memory. To solve my dilemma, I created reference cards that I use as I catalog items on my automated system. I have cards with tag numbers for names, titles, and subjects; cards for the fixed fields with their codes; cards for loan types; and so on. The cards provide quick reference at my office workstation and can be amended as needed. I also use these cards to check information supplied by vendors. After loading the MARC records supplied, I check the record to make sure it conforms to the information on my list.

— *Pat Lemmons North Henderson High School, Hendersonville, North Carolina*

Replacement Box

When I find worn books that need to be replaced, I put them in a "replacement" box for volunteers' attention. The volunteer looks in vendors' catalogs to determine if the book is still available. If it is, the book is checked out on the automated circulation system to a barcode with the vendor's name and an order is placed for a new copy. When the replacement is received, it is easy print a new barcode and discard the old book. Meanwhile, if someone is looking for the book, it is easy to find it in the replacement box. If we cannot find a replacement, I rebind the book or discard it.

— *Karen Whetzel, Ashby-Lee Elementary School, Mt. Jackson, Virginia*

Rewards for Returned Books

I save books from book fairs and gently used donations to help get our books back on time for inventory. Each member of the first class to have all students cleared of library obligations can choose a paperback. Each class cleared by a certain date receives a book for the class library, chosen by the teacher. Each teacher cleared by a certain date chooses an additional free book. Our return rate is much more prompt, and our unpaid loss rate is much reduced.

— *Pat Miller, Walker Station Elementary, Sugar Land, Texas*

Routing Professional Journals

Before we began routing professional magazines, issues often went untouched by our busy teachers. Now at the beginning of each year, I survey all teachers, paraprofessionals, aides, and administrators to find out which journals they want to see as new issues. A routing slip is placed on each new issue with a note to return the journal in three days. Teachers can get a journal back again before it is shelved by placing their names at the bottom of the routing list. Be sure to leave space in this area for people who ask to be added after the initial survey. If no one requests a title, I know we can drop that subscription. To help me remember to attach the routing slips, I place preprinted slips for each journal in front of the corresponding magazine check-in card.

— *Lisa Delgado, South Jackson Elementary School, Athens, Georgia*

Save Time Maintaining That Computer Lab Next Door

Is time managing the computer lab next door eroding time spent on library management? Do you find staff always asking you to help oversee the lab, and does it fall on you to keep track of the disks? Students leave disks out and teachers forget about disks when in a hurry. We use a system that works well to limit the time I have to spend in the lab. First, place each disk set in a plastic bag. Put large numbers on the outside of the bags for easy identification. Hang the bags in the lab using towel racks. Be sure to display a list of the software and the bag number in an obvious place so your staff can find the titles of software they want quickly. I also include a detailed guide about all the software. This includes the subject area, the grade level, and a summary of the program.

— *Robert LeCour, Columbine Elementary, Woodland Park, Colorado*

[Editor's Note: Another alternative is to purchase AV storage boxes minus the inserts from a library supplier such as Demco or Highsmith. Put all the disks in one set in the box, label the box, and store on shelves in the lab.]

Search for AR Books by Reading Level

To make *Accelerated Reader* (AR) books easier to find, I added a subject heading to the records that specifies the reading level, such as AR3.7. Now students can search for AR books by either grade level (AR3) or specific reading level (AR3.7).

— *Odile Heisel, Plains Elementary School, Timberville, Virginia*

Senior Volunteers

Finding volunteers for book fairs usually is difficult, but our community senior citizens organization provided the perfect solution. Our volunteers were so personable and enthusiastic that the book fair was our best ever. Volunteers also read to groups of children for special occasions.

— *Bonnie Rice, Path (Texas) K-12 Library*

Smarties for Smarties

To encourage children to return their library books by a certain date at the end of the school year, we stage a campaign based on Smarties candy. We post signs around the school saying "Be a Smarty, Get Your Books Back on Time." The students who bring books back on or before the final due date can come to the library any time the following week for a package of Smarties candy.

— *Beth Maiorani, Ontario Elementary School, Ontario Center, New York*

[Editor's Note: Somehow this activity begs to be connected to J. K. Rowlings' Harry Potter and the Sorcerer's Stone *(1999) which has won Nestles' Smartie Award. In England this volume in the* Harry Potter *series was titled* Harry Potter and the Philosopher's Stone. *The award is given in the United Kingdom to encourage high standards and to stimulate interest in books for children.]*

Software Statistics

To gather statistics on the use of computer programs, we ask students to request a barcoded card for each program they use. When they are finished, they return the cards to a basket at the desk. We do not take the time to physically check the cards out to the students because we "re-shelve" them on the Follett Unison circulation system. From these statistics, I regularly report to administrators and school board members. When it is time to renew an expensive subscription, I can easily check the usage figures to see if we are getting our money's worth. Our students know that usage determines what we have in the library, so they don't complain about asking for the cards. We do require physical checkouts for Internet usage as well as a log of sites visited (to be returned with the card) so we can track specific students' use of the Internet.

— *Janet Hofstetter, California (Missouri) High School*

Special Folders for American Girl

When children returned copies of the *American Girl* magazine with its popular paper dolls and related books, the dolls and their clothes were often mixed up or had been torn when the materials were stored in plain envelopes. I solved the problem by fashioning a special holder from file folders. I folded both sides inward and taped them. Then I added a pocket for the book, an envelope to store the clothes, and a slit for the doll. I labeled the folder with the magazine date and the name and number of the doll. The folders are stored, with the doll name showing, in long cheese boxes we get from the cafeteria. The children have no problems getting all the materials back into the correct folders with little damage to the items.

— *Sally Shambaugh, Guernsey-Sunrise Elementary School, Guernsey, Wyoming*

Special Mouse Pads

Some printing shops can transfer a photograph onto a mouse pad. Take a picture of the school, a composite picture of the staff, or a child's drawing and have unique mouse pads created for your school's computer lab.

— *Sharron L. McElmeel*

Sprucing Up

If you are in the midst of a remodeling project or just want to spruce the place up, invite an art class to paint your old wooden stepstools and book trucks. Our students painted each piece of furniture with images representing specific Dewey classification areas. Every summer we add a fresh coat of polyurethane. They still look great four years later!

— *Harlene Rosenberg, Hunterdon Central Regional High School, Flemington, New Jersey*

Stretching the Budget-Surprises from Your Wish List

When soliciting businesses for donations, don't limit your requests to books, magazines and videos—although such items are always welcome. Expand your "wish list." The most unexpected items can be useful. A salon cart from a hair stylist can provide storage for puppets, flannel board figures, and other storytime display items. Supermarket displays offer imaginative ways of decorating the library or displaying books. For example, imagine all your books on Hawaii displayed under a giant palm tree. Stores going out of business are a source of plastic bags. A company that has recently moved is often a source of boxes. Let local business people know that your needs range from picture frames for children's artwork to supplies for crafts projects. You will be pleasantly surprised by the items you receive.

— *Andrea Troisi, LaSalle Middle School, Niagara Falls, New York*

Stretching the Budget-Books in Appreciation

In the past, the parent-teacher organization gave school workers flowers or some other small token of appreciation when their occupation was recognized nationally, for example, School Nurses' Day, Secretaries' Week, and so forth. After library purchases were cut back for budget reasons, the organization began giving the library money to purchase hardcover books in honor of the staff person's special day. A bookplate honoring the individual is inscribed by a calligrapher.

— *Sherry A. Kalbach, Cornwall (Pennsylvania) Elementary School*

Stretching the Budget-Making Prizes for Next to Nothing: Lettering Sweatshirts

We use the Ellison Letter Machines for cutting fabric or paper letters for bulletin boards. Many teachers are discovering that the cutouts can be used to decorate sweatshirts. Simply cut the letters from fabric, apply an adhesive, and iron the letters on a shirt.

— *Beverly Budzynski, Grand Blanc (Michigan) Middle School*

[Editor's Note: This technique can be used to create one-of-a-kind T-shirts and sweatshirts for reading promotions.]

Stretching the Budget-Obtaining Atlases

Stretching your budget and having the needed materials is always a challenge. A local agency of an insurance company that gives road atlases as gifts to clients donated a classroom set of atlases to our media center. If atlas skills are part of your curriculum, you might try approaching agents in your area.

— *Mary Childs, Park Rapids (Minnesota) Middle School*

Student Check-Ins

If you're looking for ways to create time for some of the many new tasks facing you, reconsider some of your traditional tasks. For the past two years, we delegated book check-ins to the students themselves. Our students have proven they are capable. One computer is reserved for check-ins only. The students have learned to identify the appropriate numbers on the barcode label, and they enjoy keying their numbers into the computers and dropping their books into the box below.

— *Barbara Abernathy, Bremen, Georgia*

Surefooted in the Media Center

Do slick soles on your shoes send you slipping and sliding on school floors? Get out the no-slip shelf tape, cut out a circle, and stick it on the shoe soles. You'll be surefooted for sure.

— *Ronda Nissen, Spring Bluff School, Winthrop Harbor, Illinois*

Thanking the Rare and Wonderful

At year's end, I always find myself sending out repeated overdue notices and reminding students to return their books, sometimes right up to the last day of school. And then there are those rare, wonderful classes that consistently have books back on time, that seldom if ever require reminders. I wanted to thank those classes for being such good patrons, so, after the school library closed for the year, I informed the teachers involved that their students would soon be getting a treat—and why. Through the book fair company, I had received several complimentary nylon backpacks featuring the logo of a popular paperback series. I awarded a backpack to a random student in each "good patron class" after a special read-aloud. Paperbacks or bookmarks, perhaps again from the proceeds of the book fair, would also make enjoyable rewards for consistently considerate, responsible library use.

— *Catherine M. Andronik, Seymour (Connecticut) Public Schools*

Tubs of Books

Keep one or more plastic tubs at the circulation desk. When students return books, they can drop them in these tubs for later check-in.

— *Mary Ann Wingenbach, Spalding University, Louisville, Kentucky*

Use Your Automated Card Catalog for Booktalks

I inserted "Booktalk" as a local subject heading for the books on which I have written booktalks. I then replaced the summary note of the MARC record with my homemade heading. Now, when students use "Booktalk" as a subject, they get a list of 65-plus titles. I also link sequels and companion books for suggested reading. We have had several classes use our "Booktalk" function for class reading assignments. "Booktalk" also gets a workout each day during lunch as students search for leisure reading. As time permits, I am adding older fiction books to the "Booktalk" function.

— *Elli Gillum, Albany (Georgia) High School*

Uses for Bakers' Trays

Measuring approximately two feet by two feet, the plastic trays used by bakeries for storing or transporting baked goods are worth asking your local baker to donate to your media center. If you are lucky enough to be given some of the trays, use them to store maps, posters, art paper, charts and other items. Stack them to provide flat, space-saving storage for big books, seasonal decorations, study prints, and craft materials. Each class could have its own tray. Share this idea with the art teachers.

— *Andrea Troisi, LaSalle Middle School, Niagara Falls, New York*

Using the Card Catalog for Storage

When our library became automated, I decided to use the old card catalog to store the students' library cards. This worked well because the students changed classes and could not always return to their homerooms to get their cards when they needed to check out a book. The old card catalogs are also useful for storing floppy disks.

— *Cariel Thomas, Waco (Georgia) Elementary School*

Volunteer Slots for Working Parents

For many years, parent volunteers have helped in the day-to-day operation of the library. Recently, we found ways for parents who work outside the home to become involved too. During the annual volunteer sign-up at a PTA meeting, we ask for volunteers for the "Library Design Committee." Our 15-year-old library needed a facelift. Three parents met several times during the year, planning long-range improvements in the decor and rearranging furniture. Several suggestions, such as a display case and colorful section signs, have already been put in place. Proposals for other purchases will be presented to the PTA.

— *Sally Ray, Wells Elementary School, Plano, Texas*

Weed It or Keep It?

If your library is automated, you can use your computer to obtain circulation statistics that will help you decide whether to remove a book, leave it on the shelf, or boost its circulation by promoting it. Here's how. At the end of the school year, print out circulation statistics from a specific range (e.g., 000-099,200-299, Fiction A-H). Some library software packages can print out a list of books by copyright date. This feature provides you the capability to make weeding decisions without having to check every book on the shelves. If a record of weeded, deleted, or discarded items is needed, screen print the "catalog card" from the online program, then delete the record. This saves card filing and card retrieving time.

— *Sandy Nelson, Lee County Schools, Fort Myers, Florida*

Workstation Naming Ends Confusion

With our multiple, not-yet-networked workstations, students were often confused when I instructed them to "meet me at the third workstation on the left." We decided to name our workstations and our Macintosh hard drives as well. After considering several themes, we decided on popular cartoon characters. Our stations now sport pictures of the cartoon characters. Confusion has disappeared and humor (occasionally) prevails.

— *Joyce Valenza, Wissahickon High School, Ambler, Pennsylvania*

SECTION 6

Getting the Word Out
— Public Relations

> # That's the secret to life... Replace one Worry with Another.
> *Charlie Brown (by Charles Schultz)*

Well, you need not worry about it—just do it. It's fine to have a celebration in the school that will go a long way toward building a positive image within the school. However, make the celebration do double duty and call the local newspaper as well. Don't wait until you are handing out the certificates for children volunteering on a summer day to return books to the shelves after a new carpeting job—invite the newspaper to watch the action. When you hold an in-school vote for the "Star Award"—the favorite picture book or information book of your students—get permission to use the actual voting booths, publicize the voting in your school newspaper, and let the local newspaper know about the impending vote as well. Those news releases should be sent at least two weeks in advance of the event. Put the news release on school or media center letterhead.

Caption the release with "News Release – Immediate Release" and the date of the release. Briefly state the event's date, time, who, what, why, and where. Finish the release with contact name, phone number (school and home), school address (they may need it if they wish to come to photograph the event), and your e-mail address. More and more often newspapers are accepting news releases via e-mail. That option makes contacting them quick and simple. So don't miss the opportunity for turning an in-school event into an event that may also garner some community understanding and support for library media centers and schools in general. Here are some surefire ways to promote your library media centers.

A Book for the Teacher

To introduce the new books this year, I chose a book for every staff member and affixed a bookplate noting its dedication to the teacher. It was a lot of fun matching books and people. The teachers themselves were pleased.

– *Debra A. Carroll, Mt. Carmel Elementary School, Douglasville, Georgia*

[Editor's Note: An article for your school newsletter giving the titles of the books and their "matching staff member"—especially the reasons why, might be of interest to your school community.]

Annotations for New Tapes

I keep a file on my computer called "New Materials." Whenever I tape something like a new *Reading Rainbow* or the *Bill Nye* TV show, I add it to the list. I sometimes include a short description, especially if the title isn't descriptive, and I might add my own recommendation. I list the taped shows by category, and when I fill the page, I date it and send it to the teachers.

— *Margie Hall, Chapel Hill Elementary School, Douglasville, Georgia*

Annual Hispanic Events

In collaboration with the teacher of Spanish, I organized a school-wide program to celebrate Hispanic culture. There were musical programs and guest speakers. The school has voted to make this an annual school event.

— *Madeleine M. Hoss, Metcalf Laboratory School, Normal, Illinois*

Bookplates Promote Books

When new books arrive, I put bookplates recognizing a teacher or other staff member in each book. Then I check the books out to the "honored" teachers and give them a chance to read their books first or read them to their classes.

— *Gelene Lineberger, Sherwood Elementary School Gastonia, North Carolina*

Book Relays

To celebrate reading during Children's Book Week, we set up relays in the school gym. Each class picked out the items to relay for its book. We used the scoreboard clock to time the relays. Three of the favorite books were *War with Grandpa* (brush teeth with finger and flavored candy), *How to Eat Fried Worms* (gummy worms in a skillet relay), and *Pickles to Pittsburgh* (a pickle on a spoon).

— *Marion Sweany, Emmett (Kansas) Elementary School*

Breakfast for the Caldecotts & Newberys

To celebrate the arrival of the Caldecott and Newbery Award books, we held an informal party in the library. I invited teachers to stop in for sandwiches (prepared earlier) and displayed the new books around the library.

— *Sheila Miller, East Pike Elementary School, Indiana, Pennsylvania*

Bulletin Boards to Go

I have put together several "kits" for bulletin boards on the themes of visiting the library and reading. Once a month I ask the teachers if I can do the bulletin board in their rooms.

— *Patricia Kolencik, North Clarion High School, Tionesta, Pennsylvania*

Celebrate Technology!

Celebrate your successes and showcase technology. Parent and community groups will become more supportive of technology budgets if they experience what the money obtains. Once a month, schedule a parents' or visitors' day in the classroom or library media center and have students demonstrate the use of reference CD-ROMs, video cameras, Internet searches, and other technology being used in the school. For special activities, schedule more elaborate celebrations. Once our school's Web site was completed, we held the "Web Site Celebration." Among those invited were our state senators, school board members, administrators, and parents. We also put a notice in the newspaper. Classes involved in developing the site hosted during each hour of the day.

— *Sharron McElmeel*

Chew 'n' View

When I have a variety of new materials for the media center, I invite the teachers to a "Chew 'n' View" after school. The parent-teacher association provides finger foods for the teachers to "chew" before they "view" the materials. Pencils and stick-on notes are available so teachers can put their names on books, audiovisuals, and computer programs they want to use in their classrooms. Parents and administrators are also invited.

— *Esther Brenneman, Chapman Elementary School, Woodstock, Georgia*

Children's Literature Collages

To celebrate National Library Week and our statewide Read-Aloud event, students made two collages. The first collage used illustrations from publishers' catalogs to show award-winning children's books. It was a challenge to students to identify books that had won awards. The second collage featured book characters. Students developed an answer key and challenged teachers to correctly identify the more than 100 characters pictured. Both collages were framed and presented to our state senators.

— *Andrea Troisi, LaSalle Middle School, Niagara Falls, New York*

Clifford Advertises the Book Fair

To promote the annual book fair, I dress in a Clifford the Dog costume, carry a large "bone" with the phrase "The Book Fair Is Here!" and meet the school buses as they arrive in the morning. To make the bone, cut the shape (approximately 61" x 48") from the side panel of a cardboard box. As a second promotion, we baked 750 cookies shaped like dog biscuits and, accompanied by a parent volunteer in the Clifford costume, distributed the cookies and book fair reminders in the school cafeteria.

— *Sherry A. Kalbach, Cornwall (Pennsylvania) Elementary School.*

Common Vision

For media specialists or technology coordinators, the best place to start expanding program ownership is with your building's principal. Shared annual goals are the quickest and easiest way to create common visions and expectations between you and your boss. In our district, I schedule two meetings a year with individual media specialists and their principals. For the first 20-minute meeting in the fall, I ask the media specialists and principals each to bring a list of three things they would like to accomplish in the media center in the coming year. During the meeting, we establish three common goals. Progress on these goals forms the basis for the spring meeting. It is important to remember that by paying serious attention to our administrators' goals and finding ways to help meet them, we are improving the total school environment and strengthening our role within it.

— Doug Johnson, Mankato (Minnesota) Public Schools

Drawing Parents to Open House

In late September our school hosts a back-to-school night for parents. They see a slideshow about the school and meet their children's teachers. To encourage parents to stop at the library, I hold a drawing for two $5 gift certificates from a bookstore. Early in the week I give each child an entry slip to be filled out by his parents. The slip has a space for the child's name and name of the classroom teacher. Parents must drop this slip into the library contest box on back-to-school night. The next morning two names are drawn and announced over the school's public address system. This $10 investment brings hundreds of parents to the library.

— Sherry A. Kalbach, Cornwall (Pennsylvania) Elementary School

Food & Book Drives

The volunteer coordinator of the local food bank is also a library volunteer. She has arranged for local businesses and churches to donate new and used books along with food to the food bank. When families visit the food bank, each child is encouraged to pick out a book to keep. When our classroom teachers sponsor the school's annual food drive, I set up a box in the library so students can also donate books.

— Nancy Phillips, Farwell Elementary School, Spokane, Washington

Happy Birthday to Our Network

When our computer network system turned one year old we celebrated. We tied helium balloons to the computer stations and printed signs saying "Happy Birthday to our great automation system." We also baked cupcakes for the faculty and staff and put a single birthday candle on each. The celebration focused on our technology and showed everyone how proud we are of what we have achieved. Easy to organize, the day proved a big success.

— *Elisa Baker, Ursuline High School, Santa Rosa, California*

Helping the Public Library Celebrate

To help our public library celebrate its centennial, the sixth grade students submitted stories and artwork to be included in a collection of local history. Titled "Stories and Art of the People," the bound book will contain writings and photographs from community residents. To commemorate the 75th anniversary of the 19th Amendment to the Constitution, the students also gave the children's services department a collage with illustrations from more than 100 books written by women.

— *Andrea Troisi, LaSalle Middle School, Niagara Falls, New York*

If You Feed Them, They Will Come

One of the most effective ways to bring teachers into the library is to offer food. On parent conference days, we provide a "sandwich and salad" lunch in the library for all faculty members. This gives teachers a place to eat, relax, and visit with each other before returning to their conferences. We have also provided a continental breakfast when we show off new books.

— *Sue McGown, St. John's School, Houston, Texas*

Installation Information Helps Families

When students share the exciting news that their families are purchasing home computers, we give them copies of home computer installation articles and a form on which to list essential information, such as RAM capacity and memory size. We advise them to keep the completed fact sheets beside of their computers for future reference. We also provide "how-to" information for new Internet users.

— *Janet Hofstetter, California (Missouri) High School*

[Editor Note: In the elementary school, you may wish to put information about this service in your school newsletter so families can contact you for this prepared packet of information.]

Internet Training

We offered Internet training sessions during teachers' prep periods and after school. Faculty members signed up in advance for the basic introduction to online searching techniques. We then designed a certificate, signed by the principal and the librarian, for each participant. I was amazed at how happy people were to receive the certificates. Many have framed or posted the certificates in their offices or classrooms.

— *Elisa Baker, Ursuline High School, Santa Rosa, California*

Just for Fun

On days we choose, for no special reason other than we want to say "thank you" to children and teachers (and perhaps entice another one or two to visit the media center), we handout bookmarks, safety lollipops, stickers, or pencils to every reader who checks out a book. Sometimes we just put a fancy label on the child that reads, "I visited the LMC today." The word soon spreads throughout the school, and students who have been putting off coming to the library make sure they find time on these special days.

— *Sharron L. McElmeel*

Library Brochure

Create interest in your library program by promoting it with an inexpensive twofold brochure. You don't even need to buy a typesetting program. Many word processing programs will allow printing horizontally (landscape format) and in three equal columns. Once those selections are made you will have created a template. Your brochure will have four to five divisions for information printed front-to-back. Fold a piece of paper into thirds to study the layout. The first third is the title page. It will actually be the third column on the first page. You may want to include your name, names of assistants, library name, logo, school and district name, hours, address, and phone number. Inside the pamphlet use bold headings and bulleted short phrases to target key facts. Included here might be yearly statistics, available print and nonprint materials, check-out procedures, fines, special programs, author visits, book fairs, and new technology. You can purchase special brochure paper from office supply companies, or use regular copy paper. Fluorescent colors, clip art, and graphics will make your product stand out.

— *Debbie Collier, Orange Grove Elementary School, Houston, Texas*

Local Book Reviews

With help from parents, we have produced three issues of a newsletter that features book reviews by students and teachers. Called "Library Letter," the newsletter is two sheets of paper stapled together. In the latest issue, the school principal added a personal note to his review of *The Devil's Arithmetic* by Jane Yolen (Viking, 1988). He noted that he had heard his soldier-father's account of liberating a concentration camp and had seen photographs of the victims. After the newsletter is distributed, children search the shelves for reviewed books.

— *Sheila Miller, East Pike Elementary School, Indiana, Pennsylvania*

Login Screens Feature Students' Designs

My students use IBM's LinkWay software to design login screens for our network. Using LinkWay Paint, the graphics program, they can create simple, colorful pictures with holiday greetings or reminders of special school events. I copy their work to a disk and then transfer them to our network using the "Update Login Screen." It's a wonderful way to encourage creativity and build self-esteem, and the whole school enjoys the unique screens.

— *Beverly Sangermano, Quarry Hill Community School, Monson, Massachusetts*

[Editor's Note: Even the youngest of elementary students can create graphics to be used as screen wallpaper. Macintosh users may wish to investigate a simple but very useful program called Color It!™ from MicroFrontier. Visit the company's Web site at <http://www.microfrontier.com>.]

March of the Teddy Bears

For the month of October, I planned activities around President Theodore Roosevelt because his birthday was on October 27 and because the teddy bear is identified with him. Students in grade 6 researched the life of the president, compiled facts on the computer, and gave a printout to each class in grades 2-5. One day was designated "I'm Like Teddy Day." Students wore a badge on which they could write a way that they were similar to Theodore Roosevelt. For example, "I am like Teddy because I wear glasses, ...am named after my parent, or ...my birthday is in October." The culminating activity featured teddy bears. Children brought their own stuffed bears to school and entered a special parade.

— *Cindy Cox, Oakwood Elementary School Hickory, North Carolina.*

[Editor's Note: If you can, locate a copy of Helen Kay's The First Teddy Bear (Stemmer House, 1985); it makes a great read-aloud to include with this activity.]

Media Mondays

Twice a year, our library hosts a month of "Media Mondays." Teachers are sent special invitations to stop by the library during their conference periods to view new materials for their subject area, become more familiar with new technology, and make suggestions for future purchases. We invite a different grade level or department each Monday and promise snacks to ensure a good response.

— *Beth Deer, Pearl (Mississippi) High School*

Monthly Workshops Promote Technology

Many teachers are unfamiliar with videodiscs, CD-ROM discs, and multimedia presentations. Media and technology specialists can work together to provide monthly workshops to show teachers what these technologies are, why they are useful, and how they can be incorporated into exciting, dynamic lessons for students.

— *Tia Esposito, Epiphany School, Miami, Florida*

Name Labels for Teachers' Stuff

An inexpensive gift will win friends for the library among new teachers. Run off a sheet or sheets of labels with the teacher's name, the school name, school year, and grade level. The teachers can use the labels to identify their personal instructional materials and other items. Since all teachers buy some of their own supplies, sheets of these labels might also be appreciated by returning teachers in September. Buy a name stamp—last name only in small type—for each new teacher. First-year teachers will be developing units of study and will need to mark game pieces, game boards, and other items. Add a welcome note and mail the stamp to the teacher's home before school starts.

— *Melanie J. Angle, Factory Shoals Elementary School, Douglasville, Georgia*

National Library Week for Teachers

For National Library Week, I give teachers plastic book bags filled with free items I have collected during the year. I also check out a book to each teacher with suggestions for sustained silent reading during the week. I include a library week button and ask each person to wear it for the week. On Friday, everyone who returns the button is entered in a drawing.

— *Margaret Z. Jantzen, South Central Junior-Senior High School, Elizabeth, Indiana*

New at the "Lounge Branch"

It is not always convenient for teachers to come to the library to look at professional materials. We decided to send the books to the teachers. A single five-shelf bookcase is located in the teacher's lounge. Our "lounge branch" displays a limited number of professional books and magazines, which are changed monthly. Teachers themselves check out the books. The branch is well used, and professional materials are where they should be—in the hands of teachers.

— *Barbara Britton, Malabar Middle School, Mansfield, Ohio*

Newsletter Gets the Word Out

Periodically (and irregularly), I send a one-page *Notes from the Media Center* newsletter to faculty to tell them about new software, CD-ROMs, and recently discovered Internet sites of interest. I write a brief description of each and intentionally avoid categorizing by subject area so that all teachers read each description. The newsletter always draws responses from people asking for more information or for a demonstration.

— *Shelley Glantz, Arlington (Massachusetts) High School*

Newsletter Ideas

If your school doesn't publish a newsletter, consider starting one from the library. Parents usually aren't aware of the many activities in the library. What could you include? Here are some suggestions: tips for reading aloud to nonreaders and readers; sources of inexpensive books such as garage and public library sales and thrift shops; what happens during library periods; magazines for youngsters; books that feature crafts students and parents can do together; and lists of books for various ages.

— *Anitra Gordon, Lincoln Schools, Ypsilanti, Michigan*

[Editor's Note: If your school does publish a newsletter, ask to have a "Library Page" in each issue. Many of these ideas could be used on that special page. Consider creating a masthead that complements the general newsletter's masthead but will set off the page from the rest of the newsletter.]

Open House for OPAC

To celebrate our new online public access catalog (OPAC), we held an open house in the library media center for faculty, central administration, public librarians, and school committees. We draped the card catalog in black crepe paper and put an RIP (rest in peace) sign on it. In addition to refreshments, everyone received a personalized remembrance-an appropriate card from the old catalog. A few of the faculty members are authors and were thrilled to get their catalog card. Others received a card for a favorite book or a subject card related to their teaching area.

— *Shelley Glantz, Arlington (Massachusetts) High School*

[Editor's Note: If you are already automated don't dismiss this celebration idea. Celebrate the online catalog's "anniversary" or celebrate a new upgrade in your computer system. Any excuse to showcase technology in your school will pay dividends in community support.]

Original Bookmark Art

We sponsor a bookmark contest in November as a promotion of National Children's Book Week. Library aides photocopy the winning bookmarks, and the copies are used as bookmarks by other students, who enjoy coloring them. The originals are displayed in a special area of the library.

— *Deborah Maehs, Kingfisher (Oklahoma) Middle School*

Paperbacks for the Classroom

In our Spring-Cleaning Book Bonanza, we encourage students to bring in "gently used" paperbacks to donate to classrooms. All books come first to the library, and we select the ones we want to keep there. The others are divided into boxes and given to all the newer teachers on the staff. They are delighted to get these additions to their classroom libraries.

— *Pat Miller, Walker Station Elementary School, Sugar Land, Texas*

Personalized Introduction to New E-Mail Users

E-mail was new to our staff this fall. Before teachers attended a required workshop, I sent a message to every person who would have a local e-mail address. Writing 40-plus messages would have taken too much time. Instead, I e-mailed a message to myself. Then I replied to the message but changed the addressee and added a personal salutation. Occasionally, I wrote an extra sentence about something new in the library. The teachers were surprised to discover a personal message already in their mailboxes when they practiced their skills in the workshop. I also e-mail myself as a test occasionally to check how my e-mail address looks. I've been sent too many messages with addresses that needed corrections or had missing parts, so I check mine for peace of mind.

— Janet Hofstetter, California (Missouri) High School

Pictures for Student Teachers

When you are mentoring a college-level practicum students or student teachers, encourage them to bring a camera to school and have their pictures taken while they are working with students in the school. The photographs can be used to help them create experience pages for their portfolios that they will use to obtain their first job.

— Sharron L. McElmeel

Publishing Brochures

Often students want to make a three-column flier. But while formatting is easy with PageMaker or Microsoft Publisher, it's time consuming to teach these programs to students. There is a simple solution: Set up Microsoft Works, or a similar program, with columns suitable for brochures. Directions for Microsoft Works are as follows:
1. Open program.
2. Select new document.
3. Select format; then select columns. (Type three columns with 1/2-inch between.)
4. Go to Page Setup in the File Menu to adjust the margins and paper orientation. (These measurements work well: .5 for top and bottom, .25 for right and left. Choose "landscape" from Page Setup.)
5. Select location for pictures.
6. Select Clip Art from the Insert Menu. Choose picture and press Insert.
7. Go to Format and select Picture/Object if you want to use the Text Wrap feature.

— Kathy Sells, Lincoln High School, Ypsilanti, Michigan

Quick Response

Even though you may not be the district level person responsible for repair and maintenance, it seems inevitable that you will be called for low-level, spur-of-the-moment troubleshooting. These are often of the "Help! My program just locked up" or "The printer has gone berserk" variety and are delivered by a student. Just as often, you cannot leave the media center; however, it is important to respond. A short note, sent back with the student, should include the time you can check on the problem and a brief instruction or stopgap measure for the teacher to try. Be sure to follow up on the situation at the time you indicated. This may save both you and the teacher frustration later.

— Sandy Pope, South Elementary School, Eldon, Missouri

Saving Time Online

The daily volume of e-mail from LM_NET had me ready to unsubscribe until I decided to read only the first line of messages. If the first line sparks my interest, I scan further. If the message would be of interest to one of my colleagues, I forward the message with a personal note. Since local e-mail is set up for departments to receive the same message, I can forward a message to an entire department in the time it takes to forward one message. Several of our teachers have made some interesting contacts. And, getting some mail is exciting for those teachers who have not found a good listserv yet.

— Janet Hofstetter California (Missouri) High School

Sharing Free Offers

I get a lot of free subscription CDs for online service companies. I keep the disks and offer them to my faculty, staff, on students who come to me interested in subscribing to an online service company.

— Dahlia Werner, Rusch Junior High School, Portage, Wisconsin

Sharing LM_NET Gleanings

When reading LM_NET mail on the Internet, I find many items that are of interest to me or members of our staff. I open the word processing program and drop in these items. Then I print them and pass them along to the staff. If the item is a long bibliography, I print it as a separate document.

— Anitra Gordon, Lincoln High School, Ypsilanti, Michigan

Sing Out for Books

A few years ago I wrote this poem for Children's Library Week. We sang it to the tune of "Hernando's Hideaway."

Sing Out for Books

I visited a far-off place,
I helped to solve a murder case,
I won a thrilling auto race,
I found them here inside this book.
Just look.

Or if it's information please,
What temperature does water freeze?
How many germs are in a sneeze?
I found them here inside this book.
Just look.

From early days when men were hairy
and not very bright,
You'll find their learned men recorded
every major fight.
You can, you see, to those times flee,
If you will only read.

So join in this, their national week.
Pick up a book and take a peek.
You'll find whatever you may seek.
You'll find them here inside this book.
Just look.

— *Marilyn D. Anderson, Bedford, Indiana*

Snickers, Crunch, & Mars

During National Library Week and Children's Book Week, I stage activities that involve the whole school. The competitive spirit is strong in the school, and I usually have many winners and prizes. Last year I based a contest on candy bars. I put a 100 Grand candy bar in each staff member's mailbox with a note that said, "Your support and cooperation is worth a hundred grand to me!" Then I challenged each class to make up a sentence, question or comment about books or reading using the name of a candy bar. While most classes used only a single name, one class used six names to describe the library: "It's where you hear the Snickers of children, the Crunch of wild things; it's where you can visit Mars and Fifth Avenue, and where you can have Mounds of Nutrageous fun. It's the library, of course."

— *Cindy Cox, Oakwood Elementary School, Hickory, North Carolina*

Speakers from Other Lands

Public relations truly begins in the library. We brought in speakers who were natives of China, Thailand, India, Russia, and other countries for a monthly multicultural program. Some of the programs were publicized in the local newspapers, and I received more offers of foreign-born presenters from throughout the community.

— *Madeleine M. Hoss, Metcalf Laboratory School, Normal, Illinois*

Teachers' Favorite Books

For Children's Book Week, we asked each homeroom teacher to list 20 favorite books that were likely to be in our library. Teachers were asked to include fiction and nonfiction on multiple reading levels, picture books, and poetry. We duplicated the lists on bookmarks, which were given to the children in each homeroom. Each teacher who responded received a coupon for a free book at our book fair. The teachers' response was enthusiastic, and there was an increase in the circulation of their favorite titles. We also discovered that teachers were more likely to buy books when they were browsing for a free book.

— *Pat Miller, Walker Station Elementary School, Sugar Land, Texas*

The Way We Were

We created a display of teachers' and staff members' photographs as children and as adults. Parents flocked to the library during Open House to see the changes and similarities in these familiar faces.

— *Linda Reser, Iolani Lower School, Honolulu, Hawaii*

Walking the Bookwalk

In addition to a cakewalk at our school's fall festival, we hold a "bookwalk" with children's books for prizes. Players walk on a circle of numbers while music is played. When the music stops, players must stand on a number. The player on the winning number may pick a book from the prize table. The parent-teacher group provides $150 to purchase books from a discount bookstore. The store gives us an additional 15 percent off. Up to 12 people can play at a time, and we charge 50 cents per "walk." This has been a popular and profitable activity for the library.

— *Lisa Delgado, South Jackson Elementary School, Athens, Georgia*

Weekly Column

To better publicize the library and especially the Internet, I offered to write a weekly column for our school newspaper. Some of the topics have been how to get on board the Internet, how to buy a modem, online services, e-mail, and plagiarism. I also include a Web Site of the Week in each column, and ask students to submit new sites they have discovered for possible publication. Although it is a lot of work, more students have become aware of the library (and the librarian!) and its resources.

— *Elisa Baker, Ursuline High School, Santa Rosa, California*

Who Knows the Mystery Book?

Each month I hold a Mystery Book Contest by choosing one book for readers in grades 1-3 and another for grades 4-5. Each morning for one week, each class is given a clue and gets to make one guess. The first class to guess the correct title wins. On a bulletin board with a tree and owls, I attach a color photocopy of the cover of the book and a snapshot of the winning class. The kids love looking at the board and showing it off at parent nights. The mystery books are also checked out more often. To give children in grade 3 and up more practice with the library's catalog, I require that they give me the author's name as well as the title.

— *Shauna Udell, Virginia Peterson Elementary School, Paso Robles, California*

Winning Place Mats

About a month before National Library Week, our students were introduced to a contest for designing a place mat for a fast-food restaurant. The restaurant owner had agreed to use the winning place mats during National Library Week. Children were asked to use the week's theme and the dates along with the official name of the week. A committee of teachers chose the first-, second- and third-place winners. The winners' work was reproduced on thousands of place mats, which were used throughout the week. The restaurant owner volunteered cash prizes for the winners and displayed the other children's designs on the walls. Of course, many parents made a special trip to the restaurant for a meal that week. Good PR for everyone.

— *Elisa Roper, Nottingham Country Elementary, Katy, Texas*

Women's Panel

During Women's History Month (March), our school sponsored a panel titled "Women on the Move: Bridging Goals, Careers, and Dreams." Among the presenters were a physician, an architect, an attorney, and a social worker. Students in grades 6-8 interacted with the panel. They were exposed to the potential for women in the workforce, how the role of women has changed, and the obstacles women face. Research into the achievements of women throughout history continued in the library. The program will be repeated annually.

— *Madeleine M. Hoss, Metcalf Laboratory School, Normal, Illinois*

You'll Love the Book...

To celebrate the month of February, the library gave children large paper hearts with the words "You'll Love the Book" printed at the top. Several blank lines were provided on which the children could print the title of their favorite book. They could also sign their names on the hearts so the recipients could ask them about the book's contents. The students then placed their hearts in a friend's Valentine Bag to share the love of a good book.

— *Kathleen Miller, East Pennsboro Elementary, Enola, Pennsylvania*

Helping to Make Technology Work in the Classroom

> ## Computers make it easier to do a lot of things, but most of the things they make easier to do don't need to be done.
>
> *Andy Rooney*

Using technology of any type for the sake of using technology is not what using technology in the classroom is all about. We've gone past the days of using the computer as an expensive flashcard machine. Software programs have emerged as interactive programs that complement classroom instruction. We're using all types of technology—cameras, copy machines, videos, and so forth in new and interesting ways. Here are a few ways we might focus on promoting the meaningful use of technology in the classroom.

A Database for Readers

Fifth and sixth graders are creating a computerized database of books they read and would recommend to others. The students are expected to read and enter information about one book a month. In addition to a short summary of the book and their personal recommendation, students enter the type of story (e.g., fantasy, adventure), their names, and the date of their review. Only books in the elementary school library can be entered in the database. By late fall, students had entered more than 100 books. Their efforts make it possible for others in grades 3-6 to look for a "good" book that has been recommended by another reader in the school.

— *Deborah B. Salewski, Hebron (Connecticut) Elementary School*

A History of Problems

One way to keep track of problems when you have a number of computers is to compile a notebook with a separate section for each computer. In each section, keep the serial number, model number, and sources of funds used to purchase the computer. Whenever there is a problem, note it in the section for that computer. In the future, if you have problems with that same computer, you can provide the technician with the computer's repair history. You also may be able to solve some problems yourself by referring to the binder to see what has been done previously by the technician.

— *Kimberly M. Castleton, South Columbus Elementary School, Columbus, Georgia*

A Tent on a Computer

We have two computer reference stations in the media center. Although several of the resources are available on both stations, some of the lesser-used or more expensive resources are available only on one. To assist students, we put a threefold sign, or information "tent," on top of each reference station indicating the resources available on each computer.

— *Sharron L. McElmeel*

After-School Taping

When you share a VCR with other classrooms, conflicts can arise in taping public TV shows after school hours. One solution is to ask parents to tape specific programs. Be sure to check the legality of each taping before making a request. Most public television shows carry specific rights for educational use.

— *Sharron L. McElmeel*

An Address Book for URLs

Avoid URL overload and address errors by creating a file to save and organize information on promising Web sites. Simply set up a word processor (or Notepad) file named "URL." Create a blank page to receive addresses you will copy and paste in. If you are collecting URLs on several topics you may want a page for each topic. Before opening your browser, open the appropriate URL page in your word processor and run it minimized. It takes just a second to copy and paste a URL onto your page and then continue browsing. Be sure to save before closing.

— *Kathy Tobiason, The American School in Japan, Tokyo*

Bigger Print for All to See

At a workshop where two to three teachers were working at one computer, I enlarged the font on the Internet workstation. This is easy to do with *Netscape*: in the Options menu, choose General Preferences, then Fonts. Click on Choose Font and then Change Size. I found that 18 was a good font size for small group viewing.

— *Shelley Glantz, Arlington (Massachusetts) High School*

Bigger Type

When using an LCD computer projection panel or a large-screen monitor and *Netscape* to show an Internet site, make the document's text more readable by increasing the size of the font. In *Netscape 3.0* go to the Options menu on the main menu bar, choose General Preferences and then Fonts. Select a larger number to increase the font size. In *Netscape Communicator 4.0* one may access the preferences file through the edit menu. Similar procedures are available for other Web browsers. Enlarging the font size is also a helpful option to use with early primary readers or those who have poor eyesight.

— *Sharron L. McElmeel*

Bookmarking Web Sites

Before children begin to use *Netscape* to navigate the World Wide Web from our school Internet connection, we search the system and mark appropriate locations with "bookmarks." After the students have learned to navigate these locations, we show them how to move to other locations that are suggested on the bookmarked homepages. The next step is to teach students, individually or in small groups, how to conduct searches to locate sites they can bookmark for their classmates. At this point, these "searchers" have some experience identifying worthwhile sites.

— *Sharron L. McElmeel*

Building Independence

Even if you are supervising students accessing the online resources you may not always have time to immediately help each student to get online. So that no one is kept waiting, we worked out simple, step-by-step directions, printed them on a tagboard, laminated it, and put the directions beside each access computer. Now, instead of waiting for us to do it for them, students feel a sense of accomplishment when they log on all by themselves.

— *Carol Burbridge, Jardine Middle School, Topeka, Kansas*

Cache Sites

If you use a network browser such as *Netscape* and connect to the Internet via a modem connection, you may wish to cache the site ahead of time so that you are not at the mercy of the connection. Simply open the Web site you wish the students to use and make the connections to all the links that you plan to use. As you go, the pages will be cached onto your hard drive and will be accessible from the Go menu. This is particularly helpful if you are paying for online time, have unreliable connections, or simply want to focus on a finite group of Web pages.

— *Sharron L. McElmeel*

Camcorder Spices Up Projects

We use the camcorder to enhance research projects on historical people. Students must take notes, which are graded by the teacher. Then they study their notes, and we produce a talk show. The teacher is the host for three student "guests" at a time, each portraying his or her historical person. The shows are videotaped, and the teacher can review the tapes grading. Students prepare their library research with a view toward this more interesting outcome than a written "report."

— *Diane C. Pozar, Wallkill (New York) Middle School*

Classroom Management Seating Chart

With technology-enhanced classroom management, substitute teachers need not rely on seating charts in a classroom. Utilizing a digital camera and ClarisWorks Drawing, classroom teachers can keep an up-to-date seating chart with their students' names and faces. When the seating chart changes during the year, it's easy to edit the chart on computer before printing a copy to keep in your lesson plans.

— *Laura Bratschi, Garrison Mill, Elementary School, Marietta, Georgia*

Commands on the Caddies

One of our standalone computers has an external CD-ROM drive that requires a carrier for the disc. For each CD-ROM we buy, we also purchase a plastic caddy for it and label the caddy with the command words to access the program. We find this makes the students more self-sufficient in starting the programs themselves.

— *Caroline C. Bennett, Creekside High School, Fairburn, Georgia*

Computer Sign-In

In order to keep track of who has had time on the computers and who hasn't, students must sign in at the computers they are using. In this way, rather than trying to remember who used the computer at a specific time, it's there in black and white.

— *Allison Trent Bernstein, Blake Middle School, Norfolk, Massachusetts*

Copy Web Addresses

Whenever you see a recommended Web site listed in an e-mail message or on a listserv and you want to take a look at the site, highlight or select the address. Then use your copy function to copy and paste the address to your Web browser. This procedure saves time and prevents typing errors.

— *Peter Milbury, Chico (California) Senior High School*

[Editor's Note: Many of the newer versions of e-mail programs will automatically create a hot link for any URL/Web address sent via e-mail. However, senders must remember to type the complete URL, including the "http://www" portion as appropriate, or the link will not be created. Eudora and the mail packages associated with Netscape and Microsoft's Internet Explorer, for example, are among the mail programs that create these automatic links. Users who have the e-mail software and Web browser software loaded on the same computer need only click on the hot link in much the same way they would access a hot link on a Web page.]

Domain Alerts

When you are teaching students how to be selective and evaluate information from the Internet, tell them how to check URL addresses for the identity of the sources. If the domain ends in ".gov" or ".edu," it is probably reliable information from a government agency or an educational institution. If it ends in ".com," warn the students that the source is probably a business or special interest group. If any other domain appears in the address, students should look at the information closely.

— Shelley Glantz, Arlington (Massachusetts) High School

[Editor's Note: The last three-letter segment, such as "com," "gov," and "net" certainly did indicate the type of host when the structure of the Internet was first developed. For example, "edu" indicated the address belonged to an educational entity, "net" indicated a networked computer, "com" indicated the address was associated with a company, and "org" indicated the owner was a nonprofit organization. In the late-1990s, this structure was abandoned and anyone or any type of group was allowed to purchase and register any domain name. Thus, while many of the addresses still conform to the previous convention of domain names, it is not always true that an "org" domain, for example, would necessarily be a nonprofit entity.]

E-Mail Message for Students

We send a message via e-mail to all students who have an e-mail address, and explain the basics of our acceptable use policy. We also remind them of the policy when we sign them up.

— Edna Boardman, Minot (North Dakota) High School, Magic City Campus

[Editor's Note: A global mailing list of all students who have e-mail addresses may prove valuable for other school-sponsored messages.]

Each One, Teach One

To help all intermediate students learn how to compose mail offline for "flash" sessions, we used Scholastic Network's Bookwoman Literature Game as a vehicle. Each day the students have to e-mail their answer to Bookwoman. As library media specialist, I taught one child in each participating class how to compose their class' e-mail message with the answer. Then on following days that student shows others how to compose the e-mail message to Bookwoman, and eventually those students begin to "pass it on." It only takes a minimal amount of time on my part, but now most of our intermediate students can compose an e-mail message.

— *Sharron L. McElmeel*

[Editor's Note: Scholastic Network no longer sponsors the Bookwoman Literature Game, but there are other opportunities to communicate online with interactive games and quests. E-mail messages could also be sent to grandparents, parents, older siblings, family friends, and students' reading buddies. The "Each one, Teach one" strategy can be adapted in any e-mail situation.]

Eject Disks the Tidy Way

As an alternative to having students eject disks through the trashcan, ask them to use the "Put Away" option under the File Menu. Tell them to make sure the disk icon is highlighted, then pull down the File Menu and select "Put Away" to eject the disk. The icon will clear off the screen.

— *Phyllis Schicker, Purdy Elementary School, Fort Atkinson, Wisconsin*

[Editor's Note: Those Macintoshes with systems of 6.0 or above allow users to eject the disk by merely using the command "(apple) + Y" keys after the user has quit by using the command "(apple) + Q" keys.]

Encyclopedia Tutors

After teaching upper elementary students the basics of using encyclopedias on CD-ROMs, help them solidify their knowledge by signing them up as tutors for a "Tour the Encyclopedia" day or week for primary students. Either schedule tutoring time in the primary classrooms or schedule primary students to come to the library media center, either individually or in pairs. Ask the tutors to help the younger students investigate a topic of interest as they tour the encyclopedia.

— *Sharron L. McElmeel*

FAQs for Students

How do I quit the program? How do I save my work? Can I print this? Laminate the answers to these and other simple but frequently asked questions and put them next to each computer.

— *Steve Baule, Glenbrook South High School, Glenview, Illinois*

[Editor's Note: For younger students, you might consider creating the answers as a rebus.]

Fast *Netscape* Searching

Set your *Netscape* browser (*Netscape 3.0*: go to the Options, General Preferences menu) to open with a blank screen. This saves a lot of time and gets students started searching sooner since you do not have to wait for graphics and a gratuitous homepage screen to load. Bookmark search engines so students can just click on them without using the *Netscape* "Net Search" option.

— *Kristine Cole, Grace Church School, New York*

Grade-Level Options

To help students navigate through the maze of program options on your lab computers or library main menus, narrow the choices by grade level. For instance a kindergartner could type "K" to login and reach a menu of programs used at her level. A third grader types "third" and gets a more extensive list of choices. Older students have access to the entire gamut of applications and programs the server can provide. There's a variety of "front end" software available for both Macs and PCs that provides this type of customization as an option.

— *Kathy Tobiason, The American School in Japan, Tokyo*

Great Use for Scrap Laminating Film

We make use of the wasted, blank space that sometimes rolls through at the edge of laminating film by having prepared bookmarks ready, which have been made from discarded library catalogs, construction paper scraps, and double-sided tape. Our students seem to appreciate and look forward to these colorful, free bookmarks.

— *Connie Chrismore, Kempsville Middle School, Virginia Beach, Virginia*

Internet Information for Citations

As students use the Internet more and more for research, the need to know site location, date accessed, and URL is imperative for Works Cited pages. Set *Netscape* to automatically print these features by using the header and footer settings in Page Setup under File on the menu bar.

— Karen Grant, Moorhead (Minnesota) High School

[Editor's Note: Other graphic Web browsers have similar settings that can be configured to accomplish the same task. To avoid errors in recording the citation information, students could be encouraged to print the first page of Web sites that will be cited in their papers. This printed first page can be given a sequential number that can be used on note cards to indicate the source of each research note.]

Internet Party

To promote the library media center and increase the number of curriculum-related Web sites, have an "Internet" party in the media center. As an "admission ticket," have each faculty member bring an index or Rolodex card that contains the location (Internet address) of a curriculum-related Web site. Ask faculty members to include a brief description and suggestions about how to use the links on the Web site. Put the index cards in a card file for future reference. Serve refreshments. Use the party as a way of introducing the staff to the library's resources. At the end of the party, randomly select one of the index cards with a Web site to win a "door prize" for its lucky contributor.

— Andrea Troisi, LaSalle Middle School, Niagara Falls, New York

Introducing First Graders to the Automated Catalog

When I introduce the library's Winnebago automated catalog to the first graders who haven't yet learned to read, I begin with the ENTER TITLE screen. As students select books, I sit with them at the computer and show them how to type in each title. In this way, they learn simple keyboarding skills, letter recognition, word formation, and titles of books. Eventually, they confidently progress to the ENTER AUTHOR screen.

— Beverly Sangermano, Quarry Hill Community School Library, Monson, Massachusetts

Keeping in Touch with Yourself—High-Tech

I use my voicemail at school as a message system. When I'm at home and think of something I need to do or look up, I call myself and leave a message.

— Anitra Gordon, Lincoln High School, Ypsilanti, Michigan

Keeping in Touch with Yourself—Low-Tech

Write reminders to yourself on adhesive notes and then post them where you are most likely to see them—on your desk, the computer screen, or the telephone. If it's something you want to do first thing in the morning, consider putting the note on your coffee cup. If it's a job to do before you go home, put the note on the light switch. Keep a pen and packet of adhesive notes in your pocket throughout the day for making quick notes. Consider stamping some with your name so you don't have to write your name with every note to others. You could use different colors for different types of activities—or designate one color for urgent reminders. And, if you want to post a note where everyone will see it, put it on the start button of the photocopier.

— *Andrea Troisi, LaSalle Middle School, Niagara Falls, New York*

KidDesk Tips

If you have KidDesk and want your students to be able to print their work, background printing must be off. To turn background printing off, from the Macintosh desktop go to Chooser and select the printer your students should use. Click to darken the circle next to Off for Background Printing.

— *Tricia Tucker, Elm Street School, Newnan, Georgia*

Logging Overhead Maintenance Activity

We do not have time to clean our 45 overhead projectors at the end of the year. Instead, we clean the projectors each time a bulb burns out. We also keep a log of which machines need bulb replacement. The log helped us locate a "hot" plug and a defective projector—they both caused frequent bulb burnouts.

— *Pat Miller, Walker Station Elementary School, Sugar Land, Texas*

Long on Ingenuity, Short on Cash

Too few computers? Too many students? No money for an expensive LCD panel? A cheap way to give more students a view of a computer screen is to spend $10 or $15 on two extension cables—one for your monitor and one for the keyboard. Set your monitor with its long cable on a high table and ask the student operating the keyboard to scoot the chair several feet back from the table. Let as many students as can comfortably see the screen gather around—kneeling, sitting, standing. This works well for small group instruction and collaboration.

— *Janet McElroy, Central High School, West Campus, Tuscaloosa, Alabama*

Make Keyboarding Cool

To motivate students to improve their keyboarding skills, hold a contest every couple of months and award prizes to those who type the fastest with the fewest mistakes.

— *Tim Vermillion, Marshall Middle School, Wexford, Pennsylvania*

Making Digests of Digests!

To keep from using reams of paper to save digests of listservs or filling up the computer's memory by saving them all to a computer file, I redirect or forward the message to myself. Then, before actually sending the message, I edit the message to keep any information I feel is important. At this point I can either print the message, save it to a file, or send the message to myself at another mail address. This allows me to save paper and memory and keeps all my files manageable.

— *Donna Miller, Craig-Moffat County Library, Craig, Colorado*

Making Use of Free Cable Programming

A great way to increase the video collection at minimal charge is through the "Cable in the Classroom" program. Most programs have a one-year use permit. The free teacher guides have lesson plans and other support material. During that year there is no limit to the number of times the program can be shown or by how many teachers. We have been able to increase our holdings by taping from the Discovery Channel and A&E. Just make sure it is a program designated as a Cable in the Classroom offering.

— *Cecelia L. Solomon, Powell Middle School, Brooksville, Florida*

Messages on Screen Savers

Using the Windows marquee screen saver on the computers in the lab, I leave my students messages, trivia questions, or instructions for the day. Sometimes I continue messages from one computer to the next. The students love it. They are always curious to see what message will be there when they enter the lab.

— *Teri Besch, Oak Grove Elementary School, Peachtree City, Georgia*

Mozart for Learning

Standard system software for Macintosh computers (System 7.5 and above) includes an Apple Extras folder in which there is an AppleCD Audio Player. For convenience in playing compact discs in the classroom (research has shown that classical music enhances learning in most students), make an alias for the AppleCD Audio Player and put it in your Apple Menu. The application will allow specific tracks to be played, and you can adjust the volume.

— *Sharron L. McElmeel*

Name That Document

When allowing students to save their documents into a student data folder on the class computer, require students to save the document using their name and the date (mm/yy) as the title. They don't forget their own name but often forget the name they have used to save a project. Whenever they go back to the document to revise or edit, it is simply resaved under the same title. When a new piece of writing is begun, it is saved under the student's name with a new date. The teacher can clean up the hard drive by transferring the older documents to a portfolio disk for the individual student or to a class portfolio disk. With the child's name as a title and the date, a document doesn't have to be opened to identify the author and determine which document is the newer of the two.

— *Sharron L. McElmeel*

One Mail Account, Multiple Classes

We have one student mail account with Internet access. Since various classes use that same address, we ask keypals to include an identification number (which we have assigned to each class) in the subject line of each message. This way, when students access the mail account, they bring up and read only those messages with their identification number. Each student also includes his or her number along with the topic, in the subject line, on messages sent. Consequently, when the recipient uses the reply function on his or her e-mail program, the number will be in the message when a response is returned. With the advent of so many Web-based e-mail sites a classroom could have multiple accounts. If Web-based e-mail accounts are allowed in your classroom/school, please be cautioned that direct supervision should be the standard.

— *Sharron L. McElmeel*

Paper, Pencils, & Disks

If your school sends a school supplies list to students' homes, include 3.5-inch computer disks. A student's disk can be used to archive his or her best compositions throughout the year. If the student saves the documents with the date as part of the title, it will be easy to note improvement over the year.

— *Sharron L. McElmeel*

Plastic Cups As Distress Signals

When children need help in our computer lab, they put a plastic cup on top of the computer to alert teachers. Not only are the cups silent signals, but they also allow the children to continue trying to solve their problem on the keyboard while they wait for the teacher. The cups are easy to spot as we move around the lab. We use bright yellow cups and ask the children to turn them upside down. However, any solid color cup is easy to spot across the room.

— Erica L. Peto, Daniel Elementary School, Kent, Washington

[Editor's Note: One middle school in Cedar Rapids, Iowa, regularly has the computer teacher and the classroom teacher collaborating on projects in the school's computer lab. Two colors of cups are utilized. If the child needs the assistance of the computer teacher to ask a question about the "technology," the student places the yellow cup on top of the computer. If the child needs the assistance for the teacher to clarify information about the project itself the student places the blue cup on top of the computer.]

Portable Air Tanks

Tired of buying those expensive cans of pressurized air to clean computer hard drives and keyboards? If so, you need to invest in a portable air tank. A 12-gallon tank sells for approximately $29.95. These can be purchased at Wal-Mart, K-Mart, or any home improvement or auto store. Simply fill the tank and use it to blow dust out of computers. The tanks can also be used to clean film projectors, overheads, and so forth. Tanks don't have to be refilled often. When it runs out, just refill it at a service station.

— Lorrie Barnette, Midway Elementary School, Silver Creek, Georgia

Printing from the Internet Made Simple

If one is still accessing the Internet via a modem printing may be a problem if the printer does not have a large enough buffer. Simply e-mail the document to yourself to print later or send it, with a request to print, to a coworker who has a laser printer.

— Peg Weidemann, Horseheads (New York) High School

Put CD-ROM Instructions at Their Fingertips

With the increase in the number of teachers using CD-ROMs in the classrooms, I've found a simple way for all staff to use the technology effectively. A small caddy lists the directions for using that particular CD-ROM including how to start the disc and access directory information, and how to exit the program. Teachers access the information quickly without flipping through manuals, and students can progress with their work. This simple technique saves the media specialist trips to the classroom, teachers feel confident using the technology, and students gain valuable information from this resource.

— *Esther Brenneman, Chapman Elementary School, Woodstock, Georgia*

Record Discovery Channel Documentaries for School Use

Taping programs from Project Discovery on the Discovery Channel and using them in school is legal for one year. The programs cover science and technology (Monday), social studies and history (Tuesday), natural science (Wednesday), arts and humanities (Thursday), and contemporary issues (Friday). These 25-minute commercial-free documentaries are suitable for both elementary and secondary students. To obtain a free educators' guide to using programs you have legally taped from the Discovery Channel, go to <http://www.discover.com> and download lesson plans for the programs. There are also online resources linked to a resource page for each of the programs. One may also order permanent copies of the programs from this site.

— *Anitra Gordon, Lincoln High School, Ypsilanti, Michigan*

Recruiting Resident Experts

For those of us who are faced with the mixed blessings of an abundance of technology and not enough time to learn how to use it, teach others how to use it, or take care of it, here's an idea you might try. Elicit (beg, whine, demand...) volunteers from the staff who can become "resident experts" for different pieces of hardware. After all, it is not your "stuff"—it belongs to everyone. By sharing the responsibility, you can lighten the load and at the same time increase communication and cooperation among the staff.

— *Jacque Burkhalter, Fidalgo Elementary School, Anacortes, Washington*

Recycling Disks

Delete all files on demo diskettes or other computer program diskettes no longer in use. Number the disks and make them available near computers for students to use when saving data for a short time. Saves time deleting data from hard drives. We have enough available that a student can even take the diskette with him to ensure it won't disappear before he needs it again. We also sell inexpensive diskettes; students label the disks with their names and return them to the librarian for safe filing. Journalism students save all their articles, adding to their disks weekly.

— *Janet Hofstetter, California (Missouri) High School*

Renaming Bookmark Folders

In trying to create a bookmark file homepage to facilitate student access to the Internet at my school, I ran into some trouble trying to rename the folder for my bookmarks. It said "Mary Woodard's Bookmarks," and I did not want that to appear on the homepage that students would be using. In *Netscape 3.0*, the solution was to go into the Options menu, and select Mail and News Preferences, then click on the Identity tab. In the first box (which asks for your name) is the information that *Netscape* uses to create the default name for the bookmark folder. I changed the name from "Mary Woodard" to "Kimbrough Library." From there I went into the bookmark folder "Properties" and changed it there as well. Now the bookmark homepage says, "Kimbrough Library's Bookmarks." Problem solved!

— *Mary Woodard, Kimbrough Middle School, Mesquite, Texas*

School Web Sites: Is Yours Snazzy or Snoozy?

To make your site a snooze, be sure to include a copy of the school handbook, the school rules and regulations, and minutes from every meeting that occurred this year. Be sure to really put them to sleep by uploading every official school publication you can think of. You can make your school site snazzy by showcasing students' work, posting virtual tours or fieldtrips with digital photos, include launch pads (favorite educational links), information about famous local events, happenings, or disasters. You can even include school-sponsored chats via free sites such as Chat Planet. Include hot linked e-mail addresses so visitors can easily send messages to staff. Remember that your site will be visited by children as well as by adults. Is your site ignoring content for children? The last question to ask is, does your Web team include students as well as adults?

— *Bill Jordan, International School, Stavanger, Norway*

Screen Shots on Handouts

When appropriate, introduce students to new software programs or concepts by giving them printed handouts showing the screens they'll be working with. This works to familiarize staff members with new programs as well.

— *Steve Baule, Glenbrook South High School, Glenview, Illinois*

[Editor's Note: Macintoshes can capture a "screen shot" of whatever is on the screen at the time by simultaneously key stroking "apple-shift-3." The screen shot will be saved on your hard drive as "Picture 1." Subsequent screen shots will be numbered successively. Any screen shot can be cropped and manipulated for inclusion in a word processing document by using standard paint and graphic programs.]

Search Engine Rules

For optimum search accuracy, always check the "help files" or "tips" of each search engine for specific search rules that apply. I printed each set of search rules and used tab dividers for quick reference in finding rules for each search engine. This allows the students to prepare searches offline without tying up the terminal while they try to figure out how to construct an efficient search. There are too many individual quirks to keep them all straight.

— *Alice Trussell, Manhattan, Kansas*

Search Engine Site

You do not need to bookmark all of the main search engines since they are on the C/NET Express Search site (<http://www.search.com>). This site has a scrollable list of the major search engines as well as some other handy features. To get there on Netscape, just highlight and type "search."

— *Gabriel R. Gancarz, Orchard Beach State Park, Manistee, Michigan*

Seating Charts with Names and Faces

Using a digital camera and the software ClarisWorks Drawing, teachers can create seating charts with their students' names and faces. These charts will be especially useful for substitute teachers. When seat assignments change, it is easy to edit the chart on the computer.

— *Laura Bratschi, Garrison Mill Elementary, Marietta, Georgia*

Self-Tutorials for Make-Up Work

For students who need to make-up library research work, prepare detailed, self-tutorial instruction sheets for each CD-ROM database. Ask some students to proof the sheets to ensure that directions are easy to read and that no steps have been omitted. Print sheets for each database on a different colored paper; then laminate the sheets. Store the color-coded sheets in labeled stacking trays near the computers, and encourage students to use the computers independently. Following these guides should reduce the need for staff assistance.

— *Jeanne Minetree, Dinwiddie (Virginia) High School*

Sharing Disks

In a school district that contains both Macintosh and Wintel machines, I have found it beneficial to supply all users with PC-formatted disks for saving their work. The Macintosh OS can read and save to PC-formatted disks. The teachers and students who use Macs have to remember to use the 8.3 (8-character filename, 3-character extension) file-naming convention and include no spaces in the filenames because some of the Wintel machines run under Windows 3.1, which cannot use long filenames.

— *Kathleen Schrock, Dennis-Yarmouth Regional School District, South Yarmouth, Massachusetts*

Sharing Sites on the Internet

When I'm scanning professional journals, I keep recycled catalog cards at hand to jot down Web sites. When I find information about a site with potential for my colleagues, I write the subject at the top of the card, then the name of the site and the address. In the lower right corner, I abbreviate the source and date. I e-mail newly found addresses to colleagues. This has caused several teachers to ask how to use the Internet in the library, and they are beginning to surf on their own after seeing some interesting homepages. If a teacher reports that a site has changed or no longer exists, I change the card in my file or throw it away. Teachers and students are given a site card to use at the computer if they want a particular address; this is much easier than using a notebook.

— *Janet Hofstetter, California (Missouri) High School*

Signing On the Very Young

A quick way to get every primary grade child on the computer each day is to create an attendance page using your word processing program. At the top of the page, type "Attendance for (month, day, year)" and your name. As students enter the room, have them type their first name and press the return key. After they have mastered that procedure, they also can indicate their lunch choice (hot, cold, or alternate selection). When the attendance and lunch count is completed, the page can be printed.

— *Sharron L. McElmeel*

Static Electricity

Where winter brings snow, the school computer specialist knows it also brings anguished cries from students and staff: "Help!! I get an I/O error whenever I try to access a file from my disk" or "My computer (or my mouse) has just frozen again!" If these statements sound familiar, you've probably experienced the effects of static electricity on a computer user's environment. Static electricity is a familiar phenomenon. Remember walking across a floor and giving or receiving a shock just before you touched someone or something? These shocking experiences seem relatively harmless to you, but to computer equipment these small jolts are like a lightning bolt.

Nearly everything in our universe contains tiny particles of negative electricity called *electrons*. Materials that contain fewer electrons than others are said to have a negative electrical charge. Electrons travel from the surface of one material to another until the charges on both are equal. This electron rush causes the spark between the two surfaces, an electric current. *Static electricity* refers to an electrical charge remaining on a surface for a time before it jumps to another material.

Static electricity occurs most frequently as the humidity drops. During cold snowy winters, the air is dry. Heating systems remove even more moisture from the air and pass it throughout buildings. In some buildings humidity levels drop as low as five percent. Dry air and static electricity cause several common problems when humans contact the computer. For example:

> **Statement 1:** *I have an I/O error whenever I try to access a file.*
>
> ***Probable cause:*** This is caused by a discharge of static from you to your disk. The jolt hits the disk with enough energy to reorient the small metal particles on the surface of the disk whose alignment constitutes your data. Imagine the disk surface as a road. You travel on the road looking for your data. As you approach the section where the "lightning bolt" hit, you see a scrambled mess. You slam on the brakes and stall your transportation (I/O error).

Statement 2: *The stored file on my hard disk worked fine yesterday, but now I get an error message every time I try to open it.*

Probable cause: Here, the static discharge passed from you through the computer scrambling the data in the hard drive file.

Statement 3: *My computer (or my mouse) has frozen again.*

Probable cause: The static discharge passed from you to the computer scrambling information flow and causing your mouse, keyboard, or both to lock up.

Statement 4: *The printer freezes in the middle of my print job.*

Probable cause: The static discharge scrambled the data flow from the computer to the printer. The printer expects a steady, linear flow of information and cannot interpret this scrambled data. It sits waiting until it gets what it wants.

Statement 5: *The printer has a paper jam every hour.*

Probable cause: Paper is also susceptible to dry air. Below a certain humidity level, static sticks pages together causing more than one sheet to be pulled through the printer at once. Highly charged paper may also cling to surfaces inside the printer, jamming it.

Statement 6: *The laser printer copies have black streaks on some pages.*

Probable cause: Toner in a laser printer is also susceptible to dry air. At low humidity, static buildup between toner particles sticks them together creating blotches on the paper. A static charge between the paper and toner can cause similar problems.

So what can you do to reduce static charges? If possible, add moisture to the work area with a humidifier. In the work area, consider adding an anti-static mat or grounding strip to the computer or printer. Place an anti-static mat under the chair. Suggest that individuals who carry disks in their pockets purchase a small anti-static carrying case for transporting their disks with minimal risk.

— Keith Thomas, Lindsay Thurber High School, Red Deer, Alberta, Canada

Student-Made Posters About Computer Use

To teach the responsible use of computers, have students make posters that center on themes such as keeping workstation areas clean, logging off when work is completed, protecting passwords, and so forth. A poster contest could, for example, challenge children to think of ways to remember to back up disks or log off.

— Andrea Troisi, LaSalle Middle School, Niagara Falls, New York

Technology Tip

With the following exercise, you can emphasize to students the importance of knowing the names of the various keyboard symbols, as well as stress the importance of giving clear directions and following instructions *exactly*. Ask students to create screen art from letters and symbols. Set whatever limits on numbers of lines and spaces you feel are appropriate. Then, allow students to take turns dictating the instructions for creating their designs to their classmates. The student giving the instructions will learn the importance of stating instructions precisely, and the students following the instructions will recognize how essential their close attention to instructions is to their success in this and other keyboarding assignments.

— *Carol S. Davis, Dodgen Middle School, Marietta, Georgia*

Tracking Remotes

To keep remote controls with TVs and VCRs, I use Velcro to tape the hand-held control to the equipment. When the equipment is returned, it is easy to see that the control is still attached.

— *Nancy Hughes, Matthew Hanson Middle School, Indian Head, Maryland*

Trouble Remembering Passwords?

Do you have trouble remembering passwords that look like a random selection of letters? Try this trick. Select a short proverb or saying, such as, "When in the course of human events" or 'Don't kill the goose that laid the golden egg," and use the first letter of each word in the saying—in this case, "WITCOHE" and "DKTGTLTGE," respectively. It's better than putting the password on a sticky note on the monitor!

— *Doug Johnson, Mankato (Minnesota) Public Schools*

Two Computer Troubleshooting Ideas

Make a convenient troubleshooting guide and eliminate those numerous, bulky manuals. Collect troubleshooting tips for your file servers, computers, and software, and combine them in one three-ring binder. I use a separate sheet of paper for each problem. Type the problem at the top of the page and then write the solution below. File each page between tabbed dividers that designate one type of hardware or software to make it easy to find. If you travel all over the building to troubleshoot, all of your tips will be easily assessable in one notebook. I also use the binder to keep a troubleshooting log.

Second, use expandable file folders (with elastic bands) to organize paperwork and disks for the hardware and software purchases for each classroom and the media center. I keep the folders in the filing cabinet for easy retrieval whenever troubleshooting or loading new software. This keeps together a record of all previous troubleshooting problems, solutions and the date completed. The folder is a good place to keep a list of software that is loaded onto each computer as well as other information concerning the computers in that classroom. Each new purchase of a computer, printer, or software has a file for storing accompanying manuals, disks, CD-ROMs license agreements, and other information.

— *Anna Huddleston, East Ridge Elementary School, Chattanooga, Tennessee, & Judy Moore, Boynton Elementary School, Ringgold, Georgia*

Typing URL Locations

If you're not comfortable typing URLs in the "Location:" line in *Netscape*, use the "Ctrl-L" keystroke ("Command-L" on a Macintosh computer). The "open location" window will pop up. Simply type the URL there and press the "Enter" key ("Return" on a Mac).

— *Gabe Gancarz, Glenbard East High School, Lombard, Illinois*

[Editor's Note: It is often easier for early learners to utilize the open location box to access new URLs as using this option does not demand that the box be cleared first as does the location bar. In addition, the font is larger when typed in the open location box as compared to the font in the location line on the Web browser.]

Use Older Computers in the Keyboarding Lab

To get the most out of our older equipment, we collected all the oldest computers with little memory, including Mac Plus and Classic machines, and an IBM PS2 in our building and put them in our computer lab to teach keyboarding. We were able to collect enough to bring in a complete class of up to 30 students. We do not use a software program to teach keyboarding, so it doesn't matter if the computers do not match. The machines are not networked, but we are set up to print if we need to. All we need are keyboards and monitors. We teach keyboarding to every student from first grade on, so this lab is in use almost all day.

— *Linda Skeele, Western Elementary School, Georgetown, Kentucky*

[Editor's Note: Now that many schools are supporting networked labs there may not be room for a keyboarding-only lab. However, one or two of these outdated computers could be housed in a corner of a classroom to provide students in that room with much needed keyboarding practice opportunities.]

Use Students as Resources

Create a simple application form for fourth and fifth graders with blanks for name, address, phone, date, grade, and space to tell why they want training on equipment and software. Group students by need and arrange for training sessions of 45 minutes once a week for several weeks. If possible, put only three students on each computer and designate the center chair as the "training chair" to prevent arguments about whose turn it is to use the equipment. Invite students to use the equipment on their own time to practice what they have learned. After the final session, test them, formally or informally, on setting up and using the equipment. Issue those who are proficient a "resource person card" and encourage teachers to utilize these students in their classroom for help. This boosts students' self esteem and is of great assistance to teachers.

— *Sandy Nelson, Lee County Schools, Fort Myers, Florida*

[Editor's Note: Older elementary students might volunteer to also be part of a "service club" to assist teachers in lower elementary grades who might need some brief assistance during the class day.]

Using Graphics to Help ESL Students

A hopeful and motivating way to assist my English as a Second Language students uses clip art and graphics from a variety of software programs such as Student Writing Center by The Learning Company or Print Shop Deluxe. An ESL student works with another student to select and print a picture. They discuss the picture and type its English word. Using a foreign language dictionary, they look up and type the foreign word for the picture as well. As they improve, they type sentences in the two languages. Both students improve their vocabulary, social, keyboarding, and spelling skills. My learning disabled or emotionally disturbed students especially enjoy the lessons with ESL students because of their being able to help someone else.

— *Charlene Kennedy, Addison Elementary School, Marietta, Georgia*

Using Technology to Ensure Equal Class Participation

Teachers often face two dilemmas in leading class discussions. In some cases, multiple students wave hands begging to be called. In others, the same handful of students raise their hands while the rest shrink into their seats trying not to make eye contact. In my classes, a simple spreadsheet has transformed discussions into exercises in equal participation. I select a cell in a spreadsheet and type the following formula to give a random number between 1 and n at every recalculation: $= int(r \text{ and } Q^* n) + 1$, where n equals the number of students in the class. A large, bold font makes the number large enough for everyone to see on the monitor. Students number off and watch as I press the F9 key in Microsoft Works or in Excel to recalculate the number. Amazingly, students who never volunteer respond when their number comes up. It seems that knowing everyone has an equal chance of being selected makes him or her willing to speak. For difficult questions, I select the number first and then ask the question so I can tailor the difficulty level to the individual. I use the same method to ensure accountability in group activities by adding a field for group and a field for person. This way every group and every group member must be ready to respond. Using random numbers has made discussions in my class lively, and now I feel that I am giving equal opportunity for participation to everyone in the class.

— *Nita M. Rooney, Campbell Middle School, Smyrna, Georgia*

Video Output Converter

We did not have funds to purchase an LCD panel to enlarge the images on our monitors, but we were able to purchase a video output converter. The little box costs about $200 and runs across platforms. In addition to projecting the screen for class viewing, it allows you to transfer a search, interface, or student multimedia project onto videotape (with an understanding of copyright limitations, of course).

— *Joyce Valenza, Wissahickon High School, Ambler, Pennsylvania*

Web Site of the Month

Each month we select a particularly appropriate site to feature on the "Web Site of the Month" banner.

— *Patricia Kolencik, North Clarion High School, Tionesta, Pennsylvania*

Windows 95 "Scrap"

A little-known feature in Windows 95 is the "scrap." In your document, highlight the text or graphic you want to copy. Drag it to the desktop. A scrap (a file that is created when you drag part of a document to the desktop) is put on your desktop. You can now drag this scrap into other programs that support OLE (Object Linking and Embedding) when you need to. I created a scrap for my name and address, and for my URL, two things I am constantly retyping!

— *Kathleen Schrock, Dennis-Yarmouth Regional School District, South Yarmouth, Massachusetts*

SECTION

8

Technology Talk

> ## The illiterate of the 21st century will not be those who cannot read and write, but those who cannot learn, unlearn, and relearn.
> *Alvin Toffler*

While there are tricks to the trade in getting technology into the classroom, there are also tricks of the trade in keeping it there. All the technology available will be of little or no value if glitches frustrate the users into avoiding its use whenever possible. Library media specialists have a full-time commitment to keeping a library operating efficiently and in promoting reading and the integration of research skills, literature, and content curriculum. However, since the media center has been one of the first places to house computers—first for automation purposes and then for research capabilities—library media specialists were viewed as knowing something more than the others who did not regularly have access. Even now, when many classrooms have regular access, library media specialists are still viewed as being more knowledgeable—and most times because we have accepted that role, we are the most knowledgeable. Part of the knowledge comes from our history of networking and sharing information. Technology specialists have entered the picture because of their interest in technology. They, too, seem very willing to share successes and solutions. If someone has a problem, someone else already has had the problem and figured out the solution. This final section of *ShopTalk* is chock-full of ideas and solutions these contributors have probably already shared with local peers, or through online listservs, and now would like to share with you, the reader.

"Lost File" Blues

Have you ever looked for a document and forgotten the filename? If you're like me, you spend a lot of time hunting through computer files to see if one sounds like the document you are looking for. I found a simple solution for my "lost file" blues. I keep a hard copy of my files and print the filename on the back in the lower right-hand corner. In this way, I can pull the hard copy, get the filename, and then easily access the document on the computer to make needed changes, corrections, or additions.

— *Dorothy Miley, Dickerson Middle School, Marietta, Georgia*

"At Ease" Advice from Online Colleagues

Recently, a student in our lab was bypassing the At Ease (1.0) security system on a Macintosh (System 7.01) in our lab. He also gave At Ease a new password. To find a solution to this problem, I posted a question to LM_NET asking how this malefactor could have pulled this off. The At Ease security could have been breached in the following ways:

▶ Restarting the computer with a startup disk from home.

▶ Holding down the shift or control key, or both keys, while rebooting the computer and therefore bypassing extensions.

▶ Bringing in a Disk Tools disk and erasing the At Ease preference folder.

Here are some suggestions for preventing problems from happening in the future.

▶ The newer version of At Ease is not so easy to bypass. Advice: Get the upgrade.

▶ Make sure the Control Panel alias is not in the Apple Menu.

▶ Make sure the password has a numeral in it so a student cannot run a dictionary program against it.

— *Floyd C. Pentlin, Lee's Summit (Missouri) High School*

A "Reel-y" Neat Idea

Looking for a way to recycle your old 16mm empty take-up reels? I wrap coaxial cables around mine. Wrapping keeps the cables from tangling. Another bonus: the wrapped reels require minimum storage space. Microphone cables can also be stored this way.

— *Judi Furman, Hoech Middle School, St. Ann, Missouri*

A Code for Every CD-ROM

If computers in a building vary in size and capabilities, it is difficult to know if a specific CD-ROM will work properly on the borrower's computer. To facilitate teacher and student checkout and use of CD-ROMs, give each computer unit in the school a number. Similar units can be given numbers in the same range. Put these numbers on each computer. As you buy CD-ROMs code them with the numbers of the computer units. For example, a CD-ROM that requires a 14-inch monitor would be coded "Use on #13, 15, 100-199." That means computer units #13 and #15 and all units in the 100 series have at least a 14-inch monitor. Those checking out the CD-ROM must only remember their computer's unit number rather than knowing details such as memory capacity, monitor size, and so forth.

— *Sharron McElmeel*

A Free Way to Prevent Free Access

If your school is networked, you can use the power of the network to limit students' access to computer programs, files, and directories. You can "hide" those you don't want students to use and show only the files and programs they need. In my previous assignment at a high school, rather than giving carte blanche to all student programs at one time, we asked our students to log in as the *application* they wish to use. Students doing word processing, for example, have access only to the word processor files, and not the CD-ROM utilities or the telecommunications software that also reside on the server. Consequently, a student who accidentally or intentionally escapes from a program and lands at a system prompt can wreak havoc only on one application—not an entire server. This approach may not be as bulletproof as some of the commercial security programs, but it's free!

— *Carol Simpson, University of North Texas, Denton, Texas*

A Timesaving Trick with Windows

Our school purchased a site license to install *Print Shop Deluxe* on 75 computers. A network version did not exist for this program when we purchased it. Instead of taking the disks around to each computer and installing the program on each hard drive, I installed the program on one hard drive, set the printer, and then copied the program to the network using Microsoft Windows. I then went to each computer and copied the program to the hard drive from the network using Windows. This saved a tremendous amount of time. I also made a batch file so teachers could choose to run the *Print Shop* program.

— *Patsy Spinks, Paulding County School System, Dallas, Georgia*

A Tried-and-True Timesaver

You can save time by asking teachers to provide responsible student volunteers during recesses and noon hours to format and label computer disks for the school.

— *Steve Baule, Glenbrook South High School, Glenview, Illinois*

Alias Name

Many people who use Macintosh computers pull the application program icon on the desktop to easily locate and start a program. Another method is to create an alias of the application program icon and place it in the Apple Menu items folder inside the Systems folder. This will allow users to easily start a program while keeping the desktop area clean and uncluttered. If you place an asterisk at the beginning of the alias name, the Apple Menu item program alias will move to the top of the menu.

— *Matthew Clay, Carrollton, Georgia*

Bookmarks for Bookmarks

I have created paper bookmarks with a list of "bookmarks" for World Wide Web sites related to curriculum areas. Not only are the paper bookmarks handy for students at school, but the information can also be used at home.

— *Bev Oliver, Indian Hill High School, Cincinnati, Ohio*

Built-In Screen Saver

If you do not have a screen saver program on your Macintosh or if you want to remove a program that slows down your computer, use the built-in screen saver. From the Control Panel, scroll down to Screen, slide the time bar to the desired setting, and make sure there is not an "x" in the box indicating that you want the screen saver feature turned off. With this feature on, the screen is darkened after the selected amount of time.

— *Tricia Tucker, Elm Street School, Newnan, Georgia*

CD-ROM Lists

On the side of each multimedia station, we tape a list of the installed CD-ROMs.

— *Bill Sweeney, Uxbridge (Massachusetts) High School*

Changing Networks?

When we changed from a Novell network to a Windows NT setup, we discovered that most of our CD-ROMs, being of older vintage and DOS-based, would not work on our new network. If you are planning to make a similar change, it is a good idea to order replacement CDs well in advance, especially those most often used.

— *Jacqueline Seewald, Red Bank Regional High School, Old Bridge, New Jersey*

Cleaning CD-ROMs

Recently a CD-ROM that would not open kept flashing a "15" error message. I called the company that produced the program, but no one seemed to know what the message meant. One company representative said she had heard technicians talk about cleaning discs with a glass cleaner. She emphasized that I should not use a circular motion, but that I should clean it from the center to the outer edge. It worked!

— *Janis V. Isenberg, Middlebrook School, Trumbull, Connecticut*

Closed-Circuit Television System Management

Near our closed-circuit TV system, I post a weekly schedule divided into 30-minute blocks. If space permits, I post two: the current week and the following week. The schedules are laminated, and a pen with water-soluble ink is attached. The teachers are responsible for sending the video to the media center at the scheduled time. If two short videos are scheduled, I set a timer for the length of the first video so we know when to start the second.

— *Debra Carroll, Mt. Carmel Elementary School, Douglasville, Georgia.*

Comfortable with CD-ROMs

At a recent workshop for teachers who are novices at using electronic resources, I felt that they needed to have their comfort level raised. Since the workshop took place just before Halloween, I bought "silly" prizes related to the holiday. Each participant won a prize for answering a question or finding some information on a CD-ROM or the Internet.

— *Shelley Glantz, Arlington (Massachusetts) High School*

Computer Club

To fully benefit from the technological knowledge that our students have, our school started a computer club. The students in the club have helped train other students and teachers to use word processing, e-mail, and the Internet. They also update our Web site and help research new technology.

— *Michelle N. Rich, Archbishop Wood High School, Warminster, Pennsylvania*

Computer Troubleshooting

When using the phone to talk through a computer problem with a media specialist or a teacher from another building, always sit at your own computer as you help them walk through the difficulty. You'll be able see their problem firsthand and try out a solution before offering advice.

— *Steve Baule, Glenbrook South High School, Glenview, Illinois*

Computers to Go

Encouraging teachers to take school computers home over the summer is an excellent way for them to gain valuable hands-on experience on their own terms and on their own time. If your school doesn't have a "computers to go" policy, suggest it to your principal. To prevent misunderstandings, write up a simple contract between the school and each teacher about the condition of the computer, responsibility for repairs, and return date.

— *Mary Hauge, West High School, Aurora, Illinois*

[Editor's Note: One caveat. Computer labs probably won't be dismantled to facilitate the summer home use, but many classrooms have computers on teacher's desktops or in the room for student use during the school year. If these computers are also connected to the network be aware that unhooking them and restarting them as a non-networked machine will automatically cause some of the communication settings to be changed. Be sure to check with your district's technical experts to avoid problems once the computers are taken home and again when they are returned to the classroom.]

Coping with Cables

After spending all our money on two catalog stations and network hardware, we had no funds left for a suitable table with an electrical outlet. We made do by shoving one of our large round tables up against a concrete pillar, having a new outlet installed, and pulling the network wiring down the same pillar. The resulting mass of cables spilling over the table was unsightly, not to mention tempting for students. We solved the problem by spending $3 more for a 12" x 18" plastic carryall basket. The fragile network box and the surge protector fit in the bottom, the cables on top. All the cables are pulled through the plastic slats on the sides of the basket. True, we now have an ugly plastic basket on our computer table, but it's tidy. The best part is that while our students still play around with every pull-down menu on the computers, they don't bother the cables.

— *Linda Whitmore, Cedar Ridge Middle School, Sandy, Oregon*

Create a Nifty Database

I set up a database in Microsoft Works for different Internet sites that includes the site, address, curriculum area, and any special notes such as login commands. I have it open when I am on the Internet (particularly when I am on LM_NET). This way I can easily cut and paste any interesting sites mentioned into the database. I am getting quite a collection, which I can easily sort for reference and share with staff.

— *Rosemary Knapp, Camas (Washington) High School*

Disappearing Icons

Do you have problems with icons in Windows disappearing or being misplaced by the students? This tip will allow you to invoke some basic security restrictions in the Windows program manager that will put an end to these types of problems. First, arrange the icons exactly the way you want them to appear from now on. Second, hold down the Shift key, and from "File" choose exit Windows. You should hear the hard drive working. This saves the Windows configuration and writes it to memory. Next, "Exit Windows" and get into the Windows directory then type "edit progman.ini." Add the following lines to the end of the file, save, and exit:

```
[Restrictions]
EditLevel=4
NoSaveSettings=1
```

When you next open Windows you will notice that the "Delete" in the File menu, and "Save Settings on Exit" in the Options menu, will be faded out. The effects of these two are obvious. However, when you try to drag an icon and put it in another group, you will find that this privilege is no longer allowed. And since the user cannot save the settings, every time Windows is restarted whatever changes were made during the previous session will be completely forgotten and the window will appear just the way you left it before the security restrictions.

— *Cameron Walton, Carroll County Schools, Carrollton, Georgia*

Disks for Teachers

As our teachers became more interested in using computers as an instructional aid, they were saving all their work to the hard drive, which was filling up fast. To resolve this, I gave them disks labeled with their names, and I conducted training on saving files to, and retrieving information from, the disks. Once teachers had their work saved to disks, I was able to clean out the hard drive.

— *Teri Besch, Oak Grove Elementary School, Peachtree City, Georgia*

E-Mail Troubleshooter

The district technology coordinator oversees nearly 300 computers and three network servers in the two hours daily that he does not teach classes. To be fair, he asks teachers to e-mail their problems that need his attention. He uses the date and time of the message to decide who gets his attention next. Teachers have quickly learned to send their requests as soon as they discover a problem, so they will be higher on the priority list. If their computer is down, they can usually find one in an adjoining room to report the problem.

— *Janet Hofstetter, California (Missouri) High School*

E-Mail Names

When assigning usernames to an e-mail system, use a standard formula. Our schools, for example, use the person's first initial, the first five letters of his or her last name, and a number. Under our system, Becky Johnson would be *bjohns1*. If there were a Bruce Johnson, he would be *bjohns2*. This nearly eliminates the need for a published directory of e-mail addresses in the district.

— *Doug Johnson, Mankato (Minnesota) Public Schools*

E-Mail Practice

Find a friend or coworker with whom you can practice sending and receiving e-mail until you feel comfortable with the system. Don't join too many listservs because there will be too much mail to read, but joining those dealing with topics of importance to you can be helpful!

— *Peter Milbury, Chico (California) Senior High School*

Easy Access to Your Mail

Many e-mail packages will allow multiple accounts (configurations for settings) using their software. Save those settings on a floppy disk, and create an icon for "starting mail." You do not need to save the e-mail application itself if you can regularly access a machine with the e-mail application installed. By inserting that disk and using the "starting mail" icon to activate the e-mail application, you will be able to use your personal settings to access your mail. If you wish to have the e-mail remain on your mail server, be sure to check the "leave on server" option in your mail package. As a general rule, you should "remove mail from server" to avoid overloading your provider so be sure to access it from your "normal" site where you will have checked the "remove the mail from server" option.

— *Sharron L. McElmeel*

Enough Is Enough

Don't subscribe to too many listservs when you first begin. Try out a couple at a time and choose the one or two most suited to your needs.

— *Peter Milbury, Chico (California) Senior High School*

Equipment Database

A database of your school's equipment is a quick way to determine if equipment is still under warranty, and it provides a simple way to keep track of equipment purchased with special funding. It also furnishes necessary information for insurance purposes in the event of fire, theft, or other disaster. The following fields are included in our school's equipment inventory: room number, teacher's name, model of the equipment, serial number, purchase order number, date of purchase, and funding source.

— *Sue Dalelio, Downtown Elementary School, Columbus, Georgia*

Exploring the Internet & Magazines

To provide teachers with ready access to new information, we put technology magazines near the computer they use to explore the Internet.

— *Edna Boardman, Magic City Campus, Minot (North Dakota) High School*

Facilitating Repairs

If you do not have adequate technical support in your district, try using part of your repair budget to hire technical support. A local computer company provides us lower hourly rates in return for a guaranteed number of hours of work. They repair what they can on site and keep *FileMaker Pro* repair records on our computer. Additionally, they also figure out things for us and teach us a lot about our equipment.

▶ Prepare equipment troubleshooting and repair forms that teachers can use; keep them in handy locations.

▶ Keep a traveling toolbox of cables, batteries, adapters, and other odds and ends you frequently have to work with if you're called to a classroom.

▶ Develop easy-to-follow, brief directions for things that students and teachers frequently need help with. For example, we created "how to" sheets for common ClarisWorks procedures, "help" guides for copying and printing materials from multimedia CD-ROMS, and directions for hooking up various pieces of equipment.

▶ Empower teachers to be self-sufficient users of technology so they can help empower students.

— *Mary Alice Anderson, Winona (Wisconsin) Middle School*

Finding Your E-Mail

If you use Eudora on the Mac, you can use the Find command (found under Edit) to locate messages containing your e-mail name. Once all of your personal messages are found, you can start at the beginning of the mail list, scanning the subject line only. It will save time handling a lot of mail from listservs.

— *Joan Kimball, Hart's Hill Elementary School, Whitesboro, New York*

Five-Minute Trainer

With everyone's busy schedule, it is hard to find time for training on new software. I handle this problem by meeting with the teachers for five minutes at their weekly grade-level meetings. I take a couple of examples of completed work and spend five minutes showing them how the work was done with the new software. If there are no new computer programs, you could show them shortcuts within existing programs or Windows. Remember to keep it less than five minutes.

— *Kimberly M. Casleton, South Columbus Elementary School, Columbus, Georgia*

Foolproof Stymies Computer Surprises

The Macintosh computer's friendly interface invites lots of free exploration. Some student explorers are just curious. Others are mischievous and looking for ways to rearrange the desktop. In an elementary school any rearranging often occurs by accident. How can computers be protected from student maneuvers? We use a product called Foolproof by SmartStuff Software. The program locks out the Control Panel, Chooser, and other areas of the system that students might rearrange accidentally-or intentionally. It is available for both Macintosh and Windows operating systems. For more information about this security program go to <http://www.smartstuff.com/fpsinfo.html>.

— *Catie Somers, DePortola Middle School, San Diego, California*

Get the Text

What can you do if someone hands you a disk containing a word processing document, but you have no idea what word processor was used to create the document? The answer used to be "nothing." But now, with Word 97, you can salvage the text from the file as follows:
1. Choose "File," then "Open"
2. In the "Files of Type" drop-down list, select "Recover Text from Any File"
3. Select the file
4. Click "Open"

Word creates a new document containing the text—no formatting, no pictures, nothing but the text—in the file you tried to open. You have to format and illustrate the material yourself, but at least, you don't have to retype it.

— *Carol Simpson, University of North Texas, Denton, Texas*

Go Right to the Top

Getting the most frequently used programs at the top of the list in the Apple Menu (on Macintosh computers with System 7.0 or above) is as simple as renaming the aliases with a numeral preceding the actual name. The most frequently used item on most of our Macs appears in our Apple Menus as "01-Microsoft Works" and is at the very top of the list.

— *Sharron L. McElmeel*

Handling PKZIP

I've often been asked how to get PKZIP, how to install it on both Windows and DOS, and how to use it. Well, I don't use the WinZip program too much (although I do like the advanced features), but I do use the DOS version, which will unzip any zipped file you obtain (Windows and DOS zipped files). These are the files you need: "pktmzip.exe"; "pkzip.exe"; "pkzipfix.exe"; and "zip2exe.exe"—all from the "pkz2o4g.exe" version program. This program is available at <http://oak.oakland.edu/>. Maneuver to the "simtel.net" portion of this site and locate the programs you need. This is a self-extracting program, which means you need to make a directory (\ZIP is good) on your PC, and then copy the downloaded pkz2o4g.exe into that directory. Then just execute that file by being in that directory and typing: "pkz2o4g <enter key>". That ".exe file" will then decompress into a number of .exe files and other files (i.e., .doc files and so forth). For ease of use I recommend moving or copying the .exe files to your \DOS directory. Then you can execute them from anywhere in DOS at the command line prompt.

What are the functions of the .exe files? They are compression and decompression programs that allow you to save space on disks and transport compressed programs easier. PKZIP will compress the programs, PKUNZIP makes them whole again, and PKZIPFIX can fix some problems that very rarely arise with the compression process. ZIP2EXE is a new feature that lets you make a self-extracting file in case you need to send it to someone who doesn't have or know how to use PKUNZIP.

The most common usage for people downloading programs is going to be the pkunzip.exe file. Here's an easy example: Let's say I downloaded the file from SimTel in the education directory called "aalpha.zip." To digress just an instant, let me explain what the directory listing at an FTP site means by using the following example:

> **Directory Listing:**
> "aalpha.zip B 450893 941216 animated alphabet for preschool to first grader."
>
> **Translation for the above listing:**
> aalpha.zip–DOS filename for that program
> B–binary program (has actual machine language like a formatted word processor file or an actual software program; its opposite is an unformatted text file–also called an ASCII file)
> 450893–file size in bytes-450,893 for this one
> 941216–date when it was placed on that ftp site-Dec. 16, 1994
> last entry (text)–the program description

Now to continue the PKUNZIP tutorial...

1. ALWAYS make a directory in DOS for the zipped file you just downloaded. Do not unzip it in the root directory please! It may have many, many files when it decompresses, and you need to keep them separate from your other programs.
2. Now make a directory for animated alphabet called "\ANIMAT" or whatever you wish. Now copy or move "aalpha.zip" into that directory.
3. Change directory to that new directory and then issue this command: "pkunzip aalpha <enter key>" (extension letters .zip are not needed for the command).
4. Now it will self-extract, and you can look for the Readme file or .doc file to see which file will activate the new program. The aalpha.zip file has now done its work and may be deleted or moved to storage elsewhere. (I keep important ZIP files in a \ZIP directory.)

Now we know how to "unzip" a program (using pkunzip.exe). But how about going the other way–compressing files with pkzip.exe? Why would you want to do that? Well, let's say your hard drive is getting filled up and you need to gain some space. You might want to compress some seldom-used programs and just save them on the hard drive as a zipped file. (You'd delete all the regular files and just save the one zipped file that will be much smaller in size.) Or maybe a program is too large to fit on a floppy for easy transporting to another machine, so you need to compress it into a zipped file so that it will fit on the floppy. Here's how to do it.

Example A: *I have a directory called "\Splash" that is a paint program 2 MB in size. I rarely use it, and I want to compress it.*

1. Change to that directory.

2. Issue this command: "pkzip splash C: ~ splash\ ~ <enter key>." This is telling the computer to make a file called "splash.zip" and put in it all the files from the \Splash directory.

3. Now I can delete all the other files and save the zipped file (splash.zip). I will gain savings in space. Now to reverse the process I can type: "pkunzip splash <enter key>."

Example B: *I want to zip up all my .doc files in my word processor program so I can store them for safety (.doc files will usually achieve the best performance in zipped files as far as size goes. The smallest performance gain is found with .exe files.).*

I change directory to my word processor, "\WINWORD," and issue this command:

"pkzip windocs C:\Winword*.doc <enter key>." Now I will have a copy of all my .doc files in a compressed file called "windocs.zip."

Well, I hope this helped. It takes practice and experimentation to get good at PKWARE utilities. They can do many more sophisticated things that you can learn in time. Good Luck!

— *Russell Smith, Region XIV Education Service Center, Abilene, Texas*

Handy Computer Instructions

At each workstation, we provided instructions for using the programs installed on the computer. The instructions are inserted in inexpensive acrylic frames.

— *Elisa Baker, Ursuline High School, Santa Rosa, California*

Hard Copy Is Handy

It's great to work online, but those old standbys—pencil and paper—still come in handy. When exploring the Internet, keep a small notepad or tablet at your fingertips for writing notes about the places you visit and the people you meet.

— *Linda Joseph, Columbus (Ohio) Public Schools*

He Who Hesitates . . .

Check listserv mail daily. Realize that e-mail is so fast that you need to reply immediately to participate. Save the info on setting "nomail" and sending messages.

— *Peter Milbury, Chico (California) Senior High School*

Hiding Unsightly Cables

With eight computers at stand-up stations, we had a snake pit of cables hanging under the tables. To manage and hide the cables, I used vinyl rain gutters cut to the length of the tables and attached them to the wooden legs with the gutter mounting clips. We left enough room at the top to tuck the cables in. The rain gutters are not visible now, nor are the cables. We did all the tables for less than $35. Tools needed are a hacksaw or small power saw, a drill for pilot holes, and a screwdriver. If the tables have metal legs and are against a wall, the gutters could be mounted on the wall.

— *Lee Gordon, Eldorado High School, Las Vegas, Nevada*

Hypermedia with PowerPoint

Often, Microsoft PowerPoint is classified as a presentation program, not a hypermedia program. However, using PowerPoint (for Windows 95), you can use it as a nonlinear, multimedia application. Using the "interactive settings," you can define clickable areas on a slide, which may link to another slide or program, or even a URL! If you download the PowerPoint Internet Assistant from <http://www.microsoft.com> and export your PowerPoint slideshow as HTML, all of the clickable areas and URLs remain. The slides can be saved as GIFs or JPEGs and essentially become image maps.

— *Harold Doran, Harelson Elementary School, Tucson, Arizona*

ID Computers Instead of Students

I have simplified the need for individual passwords in our building by placing an ID number on each of the computers. Students can log in, type in the ID number, and go to basic programming and CD-ROM programs, as well as the card catalog. Using an ID number for each computer rather than a password for each student eliminates the need to save a lot of unnecessary files on the file server.

— *Katrinka S. Major, Fairplay Middle School, Douglasville, Georgia*

Identifying Computers and Software

I use clear plastic library pockets with adhesive on the back and library book cards to identify each computer. Stick the pocket on the CPU. On the book card I write the make, model, serial number, and county ID number as well as the software that has been loaded and the date.

— *Kate Stirk, Annunciation Catholic Academy, Altamonte Springs, Florida*

IEP Efficiency

Our county does not have computer-generated Individual Education Plans (IEP) for our special education population. To cut down on some of the paperwork and time required to prepare for each IEP meeting, we made a template of our general IEP agenda leaving enough space to individualize each student's plan. This made for a smoother and more orderly meeting. The template can be saved for revision and reprinting at a future date.

— *Rita Tyler, Sprayberry High School, Marietta, Georgia*

Keep E-Mail Copies... Just in Case

Keep an electronic copy of the e-mail you send; you may want to forward it later to another person. Creating folders for topics you are interested in is better than printing and filing hard copies.

— *Peter Milbury, Chico (California) Senior High School*

Keeping Track of Computer Changes

Updating your computer can improve productivity—or it can bring you and your computer to your knees! One method for ensuring that you remember every change or update is to keep a file in the computer. Create a directory called "Notes," with a file named "CompNote." The first items in the file should be the computer's location, the history of its purchase, and system configuration information. How much memory does the computer have? How large is the hard drive? Where and when was the computer purchased? What were the purchase order and invoice numbers? Include the sales person's name, if applicable. Other information to include in the file is the length of the warranty period and exactly what date the warranty expires. How do you contact technical support, and what are the charges? What software and what releases were installed on the computer? What manuals came with the software and the computer? This is the easy part.

Now, the harder part: every time you load a new program, backup the system, or make changes to any significant operating files, note the changes in the CompNote file. Skip a line between each entry, so there is always a visual break between entries. Type the date as the first item in the new note, and then describe any changes you have made. For example, *"8/17/94 Upgraded to DOS 6.2"* or *"12/5/94 Added a 14.4 fax/modem card and installed Delrina's WinFax."*

If you must keep up with changes to multiple computers, name the files anything that describes each computer in eight characters. (This is DOS's requirement.) And keep these notes on the computer in question and on an administrative computer. The files must be backed up regularly, as well as stored on a diskette. These files will become crucial to the smooth organization of a technologically rich school.

— *Melanie J. Angle, Kennesaw State College, Marietta, Georgia*

Lesson Plan Template

Teachers often need to write "formal lesson plans" for formal observations. Keep a "lesson plan template" on a computer so teachers can quickly type in the necessary information and print out a professional looking plan to provide to administrators or observers. You could also copy the template onto a floppy for the teacher to use at home.

— *Karen P. Eden, Old Mill High School, Millersville, Maryland*

Listserv/Subscription Organization

Shortly after subscribing to a listserv or online service, subscribers receive acknowledgments and instructions. Those initial messages contain important information about posting to the list, posting to individuals, signing off, and unsubscribing. With your first subscription to an online service, file copies of the instructions. Then when you need to unsubscribe or have questions, you can go to your "listserv" file for the information you need.

— *Sharron L. McElmeel*

Listserv Tip

On a listserv, if you're going to do something you're not sure about, send it to an individual rather than to the whole list, and then send immediate, individual responses to anyone who helps you.

— *Peter Milbury, Chico (California) Senior High School*

Mail Folders

Create folders for mail. Don't keep everything in one big "I'll-get-to-it-later" pile.

— *Peter Milbury, Chico (California) Senior High School*

Maintaining School Web Sites

Are you responsible for maintaining your school's Web site, and does your e-mail address appear when people can't find a page, often due to a mistyped URL? To save hours of replying to people who have typed in an incorrect address for a page on your site, replace the standard "error" file on your server. On the new "error" page add direct links to your server's most popular pages, as well as your main page.

— *Doug Johnson, Mankato (Minnesota) Public Schools*

Make a New Print Queue

When we added 11 classrooms to our school the existing print queues were not enough to accommodate all the new print stations. To make a new print queue, I follow the following procedure for Novell 3.12:

▶ Go to Printer Console. Highlight Print Queue Information. Press Insert.

▶ Type the name of the new print queue. Press Escape.

▶ Highlight the new print queue and press Enter.

▶ Highlight Queue Operators. Press Enter.

▶ Press Insert. Choose the group (in my case teachers) that you wish to give rights to clear print queues. Press Escape.

▶ Next, highlight Queue Servers. Press Enter.

▶ Press Insert. Choose the print server that needs to be assigned to this print queue. Press Enter. Press Escape. If you're not sure which print server to assign, look at another print queue and use the same one it is assigned. Press Escape.

▶ Your new print queue is now available to be assigned.

— *Patsy Spinks, Paulding County School System Dallas, Georgia*

Make Training a Priority

Training teachers to use the technology is too important and time-consuming to share billing with other activities. I highly recommend scheduling faculty meetings devoted exclusively to training. Beforehand, set up training stations of hardware and software as well as "training tables" of food to brighten the spirits of your faculty. Divide teachers into small groups and rotate them through each center to practice using a piece of equipment or software. Post a proficient faculty member at each station.

— *Sandy Nelson, Lee County Schools, Fort Myers, Florida*

Making Teachers Look Good

We offered a free PowerPoint class to the first 25 teachers and staff members who registered. The head of the computer science department at a junior college came to our lab to teach the class. Everyone agreed it was great to be able to take a class on-site. Many of the participants used PowerPoint presentations the next week at back-to-school night and impressed parents with their use of technology in the classrooms.

— *Elisa Baker, Ursuline High School, Santa Rosa, California*

Messages to Me

Eudora will let you transfer messages to files known as mailboxes. You can either answer a message immediately or transfer it to one of several mailboxes that you have set up. I call my mailboxes "Reply to This Message, Personal Mail to Me," and "My Target-Hits." Set up mailboxes by clicking on the menu bar and choosing Mailboxes.

— *Joan Kimball, Hart's Hill Elementary School, Whitesboro, New York*

Mailboxes for Me

Our school Internet account requires us to remove any mail downloaded from the server immediately. Sometimes when I access my mail at the school site, I find that there is a message I really want on my home computer. I forward the message to myself either at the same address or at my personal address. Either way I can download the message when I access my mail account from my home computer.

— *Sharron L. McElmeel*

Model the Use of Technology

It's always a good practice to model the use of technology as you teach others to use it. One way to model a digital or paperless classroom concept is to put agendas, outcomes, and teaching materials for technology staff development workshops on the World Wide Web. This saves paper and demonstrates to teachers a way they can implement this in their instruction. This model works especially well for workshops about the Internet.

Another good model uses classroom technology in an actual classroom. One of our teachers took a staff development group to her classroom for "show and tell" so other teachers could see how she uses her scan converter, computer and monitor.

— *Mary Alice Anderson, Winona (Minnesota) Middle School*

Modem Madness

Those of us still using modems for our connections at home—and sometimes still in the schools—no doubt have been annoyed when a program being set up does not list the modem being used. Here's how to avoid the frustration. Go to a program that you have that works with the modem and copy the modem initialization string. Now go back to the new program, select "custom" as your modem choice and paste the string you copied into the modem initialization location. The program should now work. Also note that most programs work with 8 data bits, 1 stop bit, and no parity

— *Joe Huber, Greenwood (Indiana) Middle School*

Name Each Computer

Keep a record for each computer and printer listing the type of monitor, hard drive space, RAM, extended memory, type of CD-ROM drive, and the types of different printers your printer is set to emulate. Frequently a new program will require that information when installing it. Naming the computers makes it easier to keep track of repairs, location, and the contents on their hard drives. Naming them 1, 2, 3 or A, B, C, tends to be confusing if they do not remain in numerical or alphabetical order. This is the time to be corny (as we were) or literary (authors' names). If a student needs to find a particular program and you don't have a network, he can look for the name of the computer listed by the program name on a master list of locations.

We named each computer and printer. Since our mascot is the Pinto and the media center is somewhat like a Pinto stable, our computers and printers have horse food names such as Bran, Corn, Oats, Hay, Timothy, Clover, and Prairie Grass. Each named component has a separate file card noting the pertinent information. When installing a program, we pull the cards for the equipment to be used and have them handy for answering equipment questions.

— *Janet Hofstetter, California (Missouri) High School*

Newsgroup Responses

If you use e-mail to respond to a newsgroup, make sure that you know when you are responding to an individual and when to the whole group. Double-check your addresses every time you send an e-mail message.

— *Peter Milbury, Chico (California) Senior High School*

No Address for Junk Mail

Troubled by junk e-mail? Many Web sites collect e-mail addresses of visitors and resell the names to bulk mailers. One way to forestall the onslaught of junk e-mail is to spoof or eliminate entirely your address on the Web browser. In *Netscape*, choose Options, Mail and News Preferences, Identity. Look at the addresses in the fields on the screen. If any of those are your e-mail address, every Web site you visited could have collected your e-mail address. Blanking those fields can help stem the tide of unwanted e-mail.

— *Carol Simpson, University of North Texas, Denton, Texas*

No More https

You may never have to type "http://" again because *Netscape* and *Internet Explorer* both assume that part of the URL. For example, to get to the University of Illinois Web site, just type "www.uiuc.edu." On *Netscape*, it is not necessary to type the entire domain name if the URL ends in ".com." For example, to visit the CNN Interactive site, you don't need to type "http://www.cnn.com" or even "www.cnn.com." Simply type "cnn" and press Enter. -

— *Gabriel R. Gancarz, University of Illinois, Champaign, Illinois*

[Editor's Note: Two caveats: Those sending URL citations in e-mail messages will want to include the "http://" portion of the URL as many e-mail software programs automatically create a hot link for the receiver, but only if the http:// is included. Those typing in "whitehouse," for example, will be taken to <http://www.whitehouse.com>a far different site than the site one probably intends to reach at <http://www.whitehouse.gov>. Use this feature with caution.

Professional Technology Buddies

Team with a fellow educator to pursue your technological endeavors. It can be scary out there in cyberspace. A teammate is valuable in ways that are too numerous to count. You can practice sending e-mail to one another, help each other troubleshoot problems, and in general be each other's "first responder."

— *Pat Southerland, Holley-Navarre Middle School, Gulf Breeze, Florida*

Protect Those Disks

Label all your master disks with PO numbers, vendor names, barcodes, dates, and filenames under which they are stored, and keep the disks together in a file, bag, box, or basket in a readily accessible location. When the bell rings for a disaster drill, grab the container, clutch it to your heart, and protect it with your life as you exit the building. If a real disaster occurs (heaven forbid!), your reaction will be automatic and you will save your school the cost of replacing the disks.

— *Jacque Hornsby, Unity Kindergarten Center, LaGrange, Georgia*

Quick Tip for Listservs

Many Internet beginners make the mistake of using "UNSUB" instead of the correct "SIGNOFF" command or by writing to the list address instead of the listserv address. This creates problems when an Internet provider changes an address. Those who have used UNSUB find they are receiving forwarded messages from the list postings at their new e-mail address, but they can't sign off because the listserv doesn't recognize the new address—Catch-22, Internet style! What to do? Subscribe to the list again and then send the "REVIEW Listname" command to the listserv address so the old address can be deleted.

— Russell Smith, Region XIV Education Service Center, Abilene, Texas

Quick Web Page Loading

You can speed up the loading of Web pages by opening new windows instead of just clicking on links. With PCs, right click on a link you want to follow and choose "Open in New Window." Press Alt-Tab or click on the first window's bar at the bottom of your screen to return to the original window. Repeat the right-click sequence on another link. With three windows open you can follow your primary lead in window #2 while links in window #3 (or more) are loading, and vice versa. While you are reading one page, the next one is loading, so it's ready to go when you're ready to read. This tip works in Internet Explorer 4.0 and in Netscape 4.0.

— Carol Simpson, University of North Texas, Denton, Texas

Read Subject Lines

If you subscribe to a listserv, learn to read subject lines and use the Delete key. It will make the amount of mail more manageable. Also check your disk space often. E-mail saved in folders can use a lot of space.

— Peter Milbury, Chico (California) Senior High School

Rebuilding Desktop Files

To rebuild the desktop file and improve the performance of a Macintosh, every month or so restart the machine while holding down the Option and Command (Apple) keys. On a Windows or DOS machine, go to the DOS subdirectory and run SCANDISK to accomplish the same thing.

— Joe Huber, Greenwood (Indiana) Middle School

Recording Network IP Numbers

Record network IP numbers for all computers on your network in a database and keep it current. The information is invaluable for avoiding duplicate IP numbers and to track any problems. You can also print labels from the database to put a sticker on the computer.

— *Mary Alice Anderson, Winona (Minnesota) Middle School*

Rename Print Queues to Make Life Easier

The first year we had our Novell network, I assigned print queues, numbered one through 20, to teachers and kept a record of which print queue matched which teacher. This made it difficult for both the teacher and me to clear print queues. The next year, when teachers changed rooms but the computers did not, the print queue assignments became even more confusing. That is when I discovered how to rename print queues and used the knowledge to rename the print queue to the room number. This made it easy for anyone to clear the print queue. To rename print queues (in Novell 3.12), go to Printer Console. Highlight Print Queue Information. Highlight the print queue you want to rename. Press F3. A pop-up box will appear that asks you to rename the print queue. Then press Escape. The print queue has now been renamed. You may have to reassign the print station after renaming the print queue. You will not have to reassign the printer assignment, however.

— *Patsy Spinks, Paulding County School System, Dallas, Georgia*

Reorganizing Files

After three years of saving files in chronological order on a series of disks, I reorganized files. This was the fastest method:
- ▶ Using new disks, label each like a file folder (e.g., Forms, Lists, Signs, Purchase Orders/Supplies, Newsletters).
- ▶ Insert one of the old disks and copy the entire contents to the C: drive.
- ▶ Change to the C: directory and display the list of files.
- ▶ Insert one of the new disks. Move the appropriate files to the A: drive, one file at a time. Change disks to accommodate the different types of files you are moving.
- ▶ Delete junk files from the C: directory.
- ▶ Repeat the process for each of the old disks.
- ▶ Store all of the old disks in a box marked "Originals."
- ▶ Copy each of the new disks in its entirety to create orderly backups.

— *Jeanne Minetree, Dinwiddie (Virginia) High School*

Saving Mice

I use small screws taken from my model railroad to "lock" the trackball retaining ring into the mouse while still allowing the mouse to move smoothly on the mouse pad. To implement my method, you'll need a flat-headed 0-80 brass screw, $\frac{3}{16}$ of an inch long; a #55 drill bit; an 0-80 tap to cut the threads in the drilled hole; and a pin vise, a hand-held device that holds the small drill bit. Once you've assembled the materials, here's how to proceed:

▶ Remove the trackball retaining ring and the trackball.

▶ Examine the rim of the trackball retaining ring hole to find a spot where the screw can be inserted in the retaining ring at its edge, and threaded into the mouse body at the rim of the trackball hole.

▶ Mark the spot with a felt-tip pen.

▶ Replace the retaining ring and carefully drill a hole with the #55 drill bit about $\frac{1}{16}$ to $\frac{1}{8}$ of an inch from the edge. (Get close enough to hit the plastic around the edge of the retaining ring hole.) Be careful not to go too deep with the drill—you don't want to drill into the mouse's electronic guts!

▶ After the pilot hole is drilled, use the tap to slowly and carefully cut the threads for the screw. You may find it helpful to remove the retaining ring and cut the threads in the ring and the mouse separately.

▶ Use a $\frac{3}{16}$- or $\frac{1}{4}$-inch drill bit, turning by hand to countersink the retaining ring so the screw head will be out of the way and not affect the movement of the mouse.

▶ Reassemble the mouse and screw in the 0-80 screw. Do not over tighten.

An alternate and simpler method for securing trackballs is to use a dab of super glue on the retaining rings. When it's time to remove the trackballs to clean the rollers, use a small amount of fingernail polish remover to dissolve the glue.

— *Robin Harris, Yorktown Middle School, Columbus, Ohio*

Saving Time & Trips

In their e-mail messages reporting problems, teachers are asked to quote error messages from the screens and be specific about what led up to the problem. With this information, the technician will have the proper equipment with him when he arrives to solve the problem. Sometimes, within minutes the coordinator can e-mail back a suggestion for solving the problem.

— *Janet Hofstetter, California (Missouri) High School*

Screen Saver Encouragement

Messages can be placed on the screen saver program to promote library activities. For example, put up a message such as, "Turn on to reading!" These directions are for Windows 3.1. Go to Program Manager. Double click on "Main." Next, double click on the Control Panel. Then, double click on the Desktop icon. In the screen saver box, click arrow, highlight Marquee, and click again. Then, click Setup. Under Setup, you can type your message and change the color and style of the lettering. When finished, click OK and you're done.

— *Frances Tripka, Flynn School, Perth Amboy, New Jersey*

Search Engines vs. Directories

Search engines and directories are different! A search engine index, such as AltaVista, WebCrawler, Lycos, and HotBot, is created by a computer program (called a robot or spider) that goes out onto the Internet and indexes information found on servers according to a set of criteria set up by the programmer. The information in the index is then searchable by keywords. A directory, such as Yahoo and Magellan, is created by people adding sites to a database. The compilers may use a search engine, but someone still made a conscious decision to add a site to a directory. I have created a slideshow about this topic "The Mystery Solved: Differences Between Search Engines and Directories" at <http://discoveryschool.com/schrockguide/mystery/mystery1.html>.

— *Kathleen Schrock, Dennis-Yarmouth Regional School District, South Yarmouth, Massachusetts*

Server Access

If your school district decides that staff members may access the school's server at home, including access to the mail server, you will then be able to access your e-mail from either location, home or school. The configurations specific to e-mail addresses, and so forth, are the same. You must remember, however, that the school system probably will want you to configure your e-mail so it is removed from their server once you have accessed it. If you need a particular message at home and you have accessed it at school or vice versa, simply forward or redirect the message to yourself, and then do not access your mail again until you are at the other location.

— *Sharron L. McElmeel*

Share Your Feelings

When teaching students to send e-mail messages, I always include examples of "emoticons"—symbols used to express emotions. Better known as "smileys," emoticons provide a creative, shorthand way to share feelings. Once they get the hang of it, students enjoy inventing their own smileys—a practice I encourage. Here are some examples of emoticons students enjoy using.

Emoticon	Meaning
: >)	original smiley face
: > (	frown
8-)	smiley face wearing glasses
:-0	oh no!
;-)	wink
:-D	big smile, laughing

— *Patricia Kolencik, North Clarion High School, Tionesta, Pennsylvania*

Some Rules for E-Mail

A good rule for using listservs is read it, reply to it, and delete it! Only keep those messages of importance. Keep truly personal messages personal. Talk to friends in person, write a note, or use the phone!

— *Peter Milbury, Chico (California) Senior High School*

Success Hangs by a Peripheral

In a graphical environment, the difference between success and failure depends on peripherals. I'm referring to the computer input devices—keyboard and mouse. Taking care of your keyboard is a simple matter. To remove the dust, use a flat-head screwdriver or dull knife to gently pop the keys out of the keyboard. Then, use a blow-dryer to blow the dust out or wipe it away with a clean cloth. Usually, a dirty mouse will cause the pointer on the screen to move jerkily or not at all. If you have never opened a mouse, follow the Boy Scout motto and be prepared. While it is not a complicated task, it's wise to avoid getting carried away. Here are the tools you will need:

► Clean cotton swab
► A capful of isopropyl alcohol
► Carpet

Gently unscrew the bottom of the mouse with your thumb (there's a circular opening on the bottom of the mouse) allowing the mouse ball to drop into your hand. Rub the ball on the carpet, or a similar surface, until it is clean. Then, moisten the cotton swab with alcohol and carefully wipe the plastic rollers inside. Don't press down too hard.

— *Miguel Guhlin, Mt. Pleasant (Texas), Independent School District*

Switch Peripherals

The servers for three networks at our school are housed in a workroom off the library office. Since space is limited we purchased a data switch for the three monitors and keyboards to use with the three servers. Now all three networks can be used by one keyboard and monitor leaving two keyboards and monitors for spares that can be used elsewhere.

— *Penny Peterson, Carl Cozier School, Bellingham, Washington*

Technology on Wheels

A mobile multimedia cart is an efficient use of technology. Include a high-power computer, color inkjet printer, color scanner, and digital camera. This cart can go anywhere in the building and can be used in the media center when not scheduled for classroom use.

— *Gloria Curdy, Big Sky High School, Missoula, Montana*

Transferring Documents from Mac to PC

I have a Macintosh at home and PCs at school. To transfer from one computer to another, I e-mail myself material I write at home but need to update or correct at work. At school, I open my e-mail, copy the text, and paste it in a word processing document. It looks fine, even the formatting remains.

— *Anitra Gordon, Lincoln High School, Ypsilanti, Michigan*

[Editor's Note: Many newer word processing programs have built in translators so the program can open files created on other platforms; therefore cutting and pasting may not be necessary. Simply attach the document to the e-mail message and open it at the other location.]

Two-Way Disk Labels

The problem with disk labels is that if you can read the label in the storage box, it's upside down when you insert the disk in the drive. Avoid the aggravation of reading upside down by using WordPerfect and 1" x 2 $\frac{5}{8}$" address labels to generate "playing card" disk stickers that read either way. Go to Layout, then Labels. Use center justification and a large type size. After typing all the label titles, copy and paste to get a set of duplicate labels. Adhere each pair to a disk facing up and down so that the reading orientation is correct however you hold the disk.

— *Jeanne Minetree, Dinwiddie (Virginia) High School*

Typing URLs

When you highlight a URL line to type in a new URL, don't bother pressing the backspace or delete button before proceeding to type the URL. Once the line is highlighted, it will automatically erase and overwrite as soon as you type the first key.

— *Gabriel R. Gancarz, University of Illinois, Champaign, Illinois*

Use the Right Disk

Apple's Macintosh "Superdrives" require a double-sided, high-density floppy disk. The use of other disks may result in error messages that ask for the disk to be reformatted.

— *Barbara Camp, Klein (Texas) Independent School District*

Useful Key Commands

Here are some of the most useful key commands (to use keys rather than the mouse) in Windows 95.

Command	Function
Alt+F4	quit a program
Ctrl+Esc	display the start menu
Alt+Tab	switch to the next window by holding down Alt and repeatedly pressing Tab
Ctrl+x	cut
Ctrl+c	copy
Ctrl+v	paste
Ctrl+z	Undo

— *Kathleen Schrock, Dennis-Yarmouth, Regional School District, South Yarmouth, Massachusetts*

[Editor's Note: Macintosh users will find that many of the same key strokes provide shortcuts there as well: command+Q, quit a program; command+x, cut; command+c, copy; command+v, paste; command+z, undo; command+s, save, command+m, make an alias.]

Verify Before You Reply

When replying to a message that was sent to a group of people, check the "To:" area to make sure your reply is going to the intended person or persons.

— *Peter Milbury, Chico (California) Senior High School*

Windows 3.x D S Prompt Icon

If Windows ever fails to start a DOS window after you have clicked on the MS-DOS icon, begin to troubleshoot the problem by looking for the file "DOSPRMPT.PIF" in the Windows directory. If the file is where it is supposed to be, go back to the MS-DOS icon and select it with a single mouse click. Pull down the file menu, then select Properties. Does the command line contain the full path to where you found the DOSPRMPT.PIF file? If not, type it in. Choose OK to save the changes, and test the icon.

If the DOSPRMPT.PIF file wasn't in the Windows directory (or anywhere else on your hard drive), you can create one with the Windows PIF editor. The PIF editor is usually in the Main window, and its icon looks like a tag, complete with string. Double click on the icon, and a dialog box will open. Depending on what mode your Windows is using, the box may be arranged differently, but you can find the following text boxes and fill them in like this:

> **BOX NAME**
> Program filename:
> **STATEMENT**
> COMMAND.COM
> **PURPOSE**
> Name a file that starts DOS session in Windows
>
> **BOX NAME**
> Start up directory
> **STATEMENT**
> C:/
> **PURPOSE**
> Tells the DOS session to start in the root directory
>
> **BOX NAME**
> Video mode/memory
> **STATEMENT**
> Text
> **PURPOSE**
> Specifies memory for text mode display

BOX NAME
Memory requirements
STATEMENT
128
PURPOSE
Specifies minimum amount of memory required to start the DOS session

Check the "Close window on exit" and "PrtScr" boxes. Save the file as "DOSPRMPT.PIF." Then edit the properties for the DOS prompt icon as described above. Double-check the command line in the Properties box to make sure that it accurately reflects where you saved that file. That should fix the problem!

— *Mario Guajardo, Austin (Texas) Independent School District*

Word-Process Your Envelopes

Make mail chores easier by learning to use the print envelope function of a high-end word processor. For Word for Windows, access the Tools drop-down menu and select Create Envelope ("Alt, Tools, Create Envelope"). To create an address bank of vendors, enter an alphabetical list into Word for Windows just as you would type them on an envelope. When you need to address an envelope, open the file and use "Alt, Edit, Find," then type in the addressee's name. The computer will locate the name and address for you. Then use "Alt, Tools, Create Envelope" to print an addressed envelope.

— *Melanie J. Angle, Kennesaw State College, Marietta, Georgia*

[Editor's Note: Macintosh users will find that creating a database of vendors with an accompanying "form" will allow the printing of envelopes as well.]

Working with Microsoft Works

I use the header/footer field of my Microsoft Works word processing program to save the telephone and fax numbers of the company to whom a letter is addressed. I check off the space marked "Don't print the header/footer on the first page," and the information does not appear on one-page letters. The phone numbers are saved with my files and are available whenever I have a problem. If I want a version for a hard copy file, I can run a second copy with the "Print on page 1," option turned on. If a hard copy is saved, the filename and date it was last updated can be added to the header/footer area so the matching computer file can be easily retrieved later. The *Microsoft Works Reference Manual* gives details on how to create headers and footers and how to use the special codes for filenames and date.

— *Melanie J. Angle, Kennesaw State College, Marietta, Georgia*